I0012538

Python programming for beginners

The simplified beginner's guide to learn basics Python computer language, coding project, data science, data analytics and machine learning. Exercises inside

[Matthew Python]

Legal & Disclaimer

The information contained in this book and its contents is not designed to replace or take the place of any form of medical or professional advice; and is not meant to replace the need for independent medical, financial, legal or other professional advice or services, as may be required. The content and information in this book has been provided for educational and entertainment purposes only.

The content and information contained in this book has been compiled from sources deemed reliable, and it is accurate to the best of the Author's knowledge, information and belief. However, the Author cannot guarantee its accuracy and validity and cannot be held liable for any errors and/or omissions. Further, changes are periodically made to this book as and when needed.

Where appropriate and/or necessary, you must consult a professional (including but not limited to your doctor, attorney, financial advisor or such other professional advisor) before using any of the suggested remedies, techniques, or information in this book.

Upon using the contents and information contained in this book, you agree to hold harmless the Author from and against any damages, costs, and expenses, including any legal fees potentially resulting from the application of any of the information provided by this book. This disclaimer applies to any loss, damages or injury caused by the use and application, whether directly or indirectly, of any advice or information presented, whether for breach of contract, tort, negligence, personal injury, criminal intent, or under any other cause of action.

You agree to accept all risks of using the information presented inside this book.

You agree that by continuing to read this book, where appropriate and/or necessary, you shall consult a professional (including but not limited to your doctor, attorney, or financial advisor or such other advisor as needed) before using any of the suggested remedies, techniques, or information in this book.

Table of Contents

5

Chapter 1:What is Python?

What is Python?

Python is an awesome decision on machine learning for a few reasons. Most importantly, it's a basic dialect at first glance. Regardless of whether you're not acquainted with Python, getting up to speed is snappy in the event that you at any point have utilized some other dialect with C-like grammar.

Second, Python has an incredible network which results in great documentation and inviting and extensive answers in StackOverflow (central!).

Third, coming from the colossal network, there are a lot of valuable libraries for Python (both as "batteries included" an outsider), which take care of essentially any issue that you can have (counting machine learning).

Wait I thought this machine language was slow?

Unfortunately, it is a very valid question that deserves an answer. Indeed, Python is not at all the fastest language on the planet.

However, here's the caveat: libraries can and do offload the costly computations to the substantially more performant (yet much harder to use) C and C++ are prime examples. There's NumPy, which is a library for numerical calculation. It is composed in C, and it's quick. For all intents and purposes, each library out there that includes serious estimations utilizes it—every one of the libraries recorded next utilize it in some shape. On the off chance that you read NumPy, think quick.

In this way, you can influence your computer scripts to run essentially as quick as handwriting them out in a lower level dialect. So there's truly nothing to stress over with regards to speed and agility.

If you want to know which Python libraries you should check out. Try some of these.

"Scikit-learn"

Do you need something that completely addresses everything from testing and training models to engineering techniques?

Then scikit-learn is your best solution. This incredible bit of free programming gives each device important to machine learning and information mining. It's the true standard library for machine learning in Python; suggested for the vast majority of the 'old' ML calculations.

This library does both characterization and relapse, supporting essentially every calculation out there (bolster vector machines, arbitrary timberland, Bayes, you name it). It allows a simple exchanging of calculations in which experimentation is a lot simpler. These 'more seasoned' calculations are shockingly flexible and work extremely well in a considerable amount of problems and case studies.

In any case, that is not all! Scikit-learn additionally does groupings, plural dimensionalities, and so on. It's likewise exceedingly quick since it keeps running on NumPy and SciPy.

Look at a few cases to see everything this library is prepared to do, the instructional exercises on the website, and the need to figure out if this is a good fit.

"NLTK"

While not a machine learning library essentially, NLTK is an unquestionable requirement when working with regular computer language. It is bundled with a heap of Datasets and other rhetorical data assets, which is invaluable for preparing certain models. Aside from the libraries for working with content, this is great for determining capacities, for example, characterization, tokenization, stemming, labeling, and parsing—that's just the beginning.

The handiness of having the majority of this stuff perfectly bundled can't be exaggerated. In case you are keen on regular computer language look at a few of their website's instructional exercises!

"Theano"

Utilized generally in research and within the scholarly community, Theano is the granddad of all deeply profound learning systems. Since it is written in Python, it is firmly incorporated with NumPy. Theano enables you to make neural systems which are essential scientific articulations with multi-dimensional clusters. Theano handles this so you that you don't need to stress over the real usage of the math included.

It bolsters offloading figures to a considerably speedier GPU, which is an element that everybody underpins today, yet, back when they presented it, this wasn't the situation. The library is extremely developed now and boasts an extensive variety of activities, which is extraordinary with regards to contrasting it and other comparative libraries.

The greatest grievance out there about Theano is the API might be cumbersome for a few, making the library difficult to use for beginning learners. In any case, there are tools that relieve the agony and makes working with Theano pretty straightforward, for example, try using Keras, or Blocks, and even Lasagne.

"TensorFlow"

The geniuses over at Google made TensorFlow for inside use in machine learning applications and publicly released it in late 2015. They needed something that could supplant their more established, non-open source machine learning structure, **DistBelief**. It wasn't sufficiently adaptable and too firmly ingrained into their foundation. It was to be imparted to different analysts around the globe.

Thus, TensorFlow was made. Despite their slip-ups in the past, many view this library as a much-needed change over Theano, asserting greater adaptability and more instinctive API. Another great benefit is it can be utilized to create new conditions, supporting tremendous amounts of new GPUs for training and learning purposes. While it doesn't bolster as wide a scope of functionality like Theano, it has better computational diagram representations.

TensorFlow is exceptionally famous these days. In fact, if you are familiar with every single library on this list, you can agree that there has been a huge influx in the number of new users and bloggers in this library and its functionality. This is definitely a good thing for beginners.

"Keras"

Keras is a phenomenal library that gives a top-level API to neural systems and is best for running alongside or on top of Theano or TensorFlow. It makes bridling full intensity of these intricate bits of programming substantially simpler than utilizing them all by themselves. The greatest benefit of this library is its exceptional ease of understanding, putting the end users' needs and experiences as its number one priority. This cuts down on a number of errors.

It is also secluded; which means that individual models like neural layers and cost capacities can be grouped together with little to no limitations. This additionally makes the library simple to include new models and interface them with the current ones.

A few people have called Keras great that it is similar to cheating on your exam. In case you're beginning with higher learning in this area, take the illustrations and examples and discover what you can do with it. Try exploring.

Furthermore, by chance that you need to START learning, it is recommended that you begin with their instructional exercises and see where you can go from that point.

Two comparative choices are Lasagne and Blocks; however, they just keep running on Theano. If you attempted Keras and have difficulty, perhaps, experiment with one of these contrasting options to check whether they work out for you.

"PyTorch"

If you are looking for a popular deep learning library, then look no further than Torch, which is written in the language called Lua. Facebook recently open-sourced a Python model of Torch and named it PyTorch, which allows you to easily use the exact same libraries that Torch uses, but from Python, instead of the original language, Lua.

PyTorch is significantly easier for debugging because of one major difference between Theano, TensorFlow, and PyTorch. The older versions use allegorical computation while the newer does not. Allegorical computation is simply a way of saying that coding an operation, for example, 'a + b', will not be computed when that line is read. Before it is executed it must be translated into what is called CUDA or C. This makes the debugging much harder to execute in Theano/TensorFlow since this error is more difficult to pinpoint with a specific line of code. It's basically harder to trace back to the source. Debugging is not one of this library's strongest features.

This is extremely beginner-friendly; as your learning increases, try some of their more advanced tutorials and examples.

History of Python

Python was invented in the later years of the 1980s. Guido van Rossum, the founder, started using the language in December 1989. He is Python's only known creator and his integral role in the growth and development of the language has earned him the nickname "Benevolent Dictator for Life". It was created to be the successor to the language known as ABC.

The next version that was released was Python 2.0, in October of the year 2000 and had significant upgrades and new highlights, including a cycle-distinguishing junk jockey and back up support for Unicode. It was most fortunate, that this particular version, made vast improvement procedures to the language turned out to be more straightforward and network sponsored.

Python 3.0, which initially started its existence as Py3K. Funny right? This version was rolled out in December of 2008 after a rigorous testing period. This particular version of Python was hard to roll back to previous compatible versions which are the most unfortunate. Yet, a significant number of its real highlights have been rolled back to versions 2.6 or 2.7 (Python), and rollouts of Python 3 which utilizes the two to three utilities, that helps to automate the interpretation of the Python script.

Python 2.7's expiry date was originally supposed to be back in 2015, but for unidentifiable reasons, it was put off until the year 2020. It was known that there was a major concern about data being unable to roll back but roll FORWARD into the new version, Python 3. In 2017, Google declared that there would be work done on Python 2.7 to enhance execution under simultaneously running tasks.

Different of Python version

There are going to be times that the version of Python that is being used is not the version that you want your program to be executed in due to the fact that it is a version of Python that is less supported or because you think that having a different version of Python is going to cause the program to run in a different manner, and you want to see what it would do in that version. But, how are you going to be able to tell which version of Python you are using before you execute your program?

With this bit of code, you are going to be able to figure out which version of Python you are using in a block of code that is readable to you as a programmer.

Four Ways to Reverse Strings and Lists

You are going to have four different ways that you can reverse the order of your strings or lists depending on what your end goal is. You are going to do this whenever it comes to fixing a mistake that you may have made, or to get a different result than what you got in the first place.

Method one: Reversing the list within itself.

With this method, you are going to be taking the list itself and changing it with a simple line of code.

Example

Sample line = [4, 2, 5]

Sample line. Reverse ()

Print (sample line)

-> [5, 3, 4]

Fairly straightforward right? All you are doing is studying the list that you have created in Python and flipping it around by reading it from the end of the line to the beginning.

Method two: Iterating within a loop

When you are iterating inside of a loop, you are still going to be reversing your list, but instead, you are going to be doing it inside of a loop which is going to cause your list to be printed out one element at a time.

Example

For object in reverse ([5, 6, 2]): print (objects)

1 -> 2

2 -> 6

3 -> 5

Method three: reverse a string inside of a line

Whenever you modify a string inside of a line, you are going to get the same result that you have been getting with the other examples that you have seen in this chapter. However, if you do not have any objects inside of that string, then you are going to be getting a different result than what you may be expecting.

Example

"Sample line" [: : -1]

Enil elpmaS

A little different correct? Well, that is alright because either way, you are getting the reversed order of your string in the line that it is occupying.

Method four: Reversing a string by using the slicing method

You have used slicing to slice the indexes for strings, lists, and tuples. But, you can also use that same method to reverse the order of a string. It is going to work the same way that you would slice an index, and you are still going to get the reverse order of the string that you have created. The code is gong to look similar to the code that you just used in method three.

[3, 1, 5] [: : -1]

Result: 5, 1, 3

So, no matter which way you use it, you are going to be getting the reverse order of your lines and strings when you use the reverse code. It is going to depend on what you are trying to accomplish in order to determine which method is going to be right for you.

You may want to practice each of these methods so that you are able to get familiar with them and understand how they work.

Chapter 2:Installation of Python

How to download and install(different O.S.) Python;

Steps in downloading Python 2.7.12, and installing it on Windows

1. Type python on your browser and press the Search button to display the search results.

Scroll down to find the item you are interested in. In this instance, you are looking for python. click "python releases for windows", and a new page opens. See image below:

2. Select the Python version, python 2.7.12, and click, or you can select the version that is compatible to your device or OS.

Python Releases for Windows

- Latest Python 2 Release - Python 2.7.12
- Latest Python 3 Release - Python 3.5.2

- Python 3.6.0b1 - 2016-09-12
  - Download Windows x86 web-based installer
  - Download Windows x86 executable installer
  - Download Windows x86 embeddable zip file
  - Download Windows x86-64 web-based installer
  - Download Windows x86-64 executable installer
  - Download Windows x86-64 embeddable zip file
  - Download Windows help file
- Python 3.6.0a4 - 2016-08-15
  - Download Windows x86 web-based installer
  - Download Windows x86 executable installer
  - Download Windows x86 embeddable zip file
  - Download Windows x86-64 web-based installer
  - Download Windows x86-64 executable installer
  - Download Windows x86-64 embeddable zip file

3. The new page contains the various python types. Scroll down and select an option: in this instance, select Windows x86 MSI installer and click.

4. Press the Python box at the bottom of your screen.

Click the "Run" button, and wait for the new window to appear.

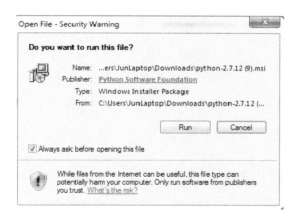

5. Select the user options that you require and press "NEXT".

Your screen will display the hard drive where your python will be located.

6. Press the "NEXT" button.

7. Press yes, and wait for a few minutes. Sometimes it can take longer for the application to download, depending on the speed of your internet.

8. After that, click the FINISHED button to signify that the installation has been completed

Your python has been installed in your computer and is now ready to use. Find it in drive C, or wherever you have saved it.

There can be glitches along the way, but there are options which are presented in this article. If you follow it well, there is no reason that you cannot perform this task.

It's important to note that there's no need to compile programs. Python is an interpretive language and can execute quickly your commands.

You can also download directly from the Python website, by selecting any of these versions – 3.5.2 or 2.7.12. and clicking 'download'. (For this book, 2.7.12 is used, in general, for easy discussions).

See image below:

Follow the step by step instructions prompted by the program itself. Save and run the program in your computer.

For Mac

To download Python on Mac, you can follow a similar procedure, but this time, you will have to access the "Python.mpkg" file, to run the installer.

For Linux

For Linux, Python 2 and 3 may have been installed by default. Hence, check first your operating system. You can check if your device has already a Python program, by accessing your command prompt and entering this: python—version, or python3—version.

If Python is not installed in your Linux, the result "command not found" will be displayed. You may want to download both Python 2.7.12 and any of the versions of Python 3 for your Linux. This is due to the fact that Linux can have more compatibility with Python 3.

For windows users, now that you have downloaded the program, you're ready to start.

And yes, congratulations! You can now begin working and having fun with your Python programming system.

Before you can start programming, you need to download and install Python on your machine. The installation is quite straightforward no matter what operating system you're running, however you do need to pay attention to a couple of things.

First, you need to head to Python's homepage at www.python.org and head to the "Downloads" section.

There you will see a number of different installers and each one of them has a different version. Make sure to download the right installer that matches your computer's operating system and select the latest version.

Once the download is complete, run the installer and follow the steps. You should simply accept the standard settings and once the installation is complete, you're ready to go.

If for some reason you don't want to install Python, you may notice that on the website's homepage you have some kind of a console. This is a Python online console and you can use it to practice your coding skills, or to try out some of the examples in this book. It's advisable for you to type the code yourself, even if you copy it from the book, and then try to be creative with it. You need to practice in order to memorize the syntax and specific commands, and the online console is really handy for a quick practice session.

Using a Text Editor

Python programming can be done with nearly any kind of plain text editor. You can use programs like Notepad, Notepad++, gedit, and many more. Keep in mind that some of these text editors come with a variety of features that are useful to programmers. For instance some of them, such as Notepad++ offer syntax highlighting which will instantly show you any errors you made. If you type code in a basic editor like plain Notepad, the program won't tell you when you've forgotten a semicolon or if you added additional space. There are many programs to choose from, so pick any editor you feel comfortable with.

With that in mind, avoid using word processors such as Microsoft Word or Open Office. They aren't good for programming purposes. They can be used to write code, however the problem is that when saving it the program will sneak in some additional lines of code by itself. That code is specific to the word processor and it can impact your program's speed, or even worse, it will simply not run.

Preparing computer for Python;

Now that your toolkit is prepared, it's time to write your first program. For this example we'll use IDLE because it's important to get used to IDE's from the start in order to avoid any future frustrations. If you prefer to use a text editor or the online Python console, go ahead, the code will work the same.

Now, start running IDLE in interactive mode. You will now see a window that is known as a Python shell. At the command prompt type the following line:

```
print ("Hello World!")
```

Now you should see the result displayed on your screen as the following: Hello World!

That's it! Congratulations, you can call yourself a programmer now. Now let's discuss this bit of code briefly. The first thing you'll notice is that Python code is plain English, easy to read and understand. Even without programming knowledge, you probably knew what this line of code would do because it's self-explanatory. That's the beauty of working with Python.

As for the command we used, "print ()" is a function that displays the text which is written in the parentheses. Keep in mind that the line needs to be surrounded by quotation marks, otherwise you'll get an error. Furthermore, pay attention to how you type the function because in Python everything is case sensitive. The command "print" will work, however if you type it as "Print" it will not.

Now, let's create the same program but this time by using IDLE's script mode. Don't forget that interactive mode gives you instant results. It works the same as the online Python shell. However, you won't be able to save your program so that you can continue working on it later. In order to save it and edit it later, you need to work in script mode. You can run IDLE in script mode simply by clicking on "File" and selecting "New Window". Now type the same line again:

print ("Hello World!)

Hit the Enter key. You'll notice that nothing happens. That's because you are writing a list of instructions that will be executed at a later date when you run the program. First, you need to save the application by clicking on "Save As" from the "File" menu. You'll notice that by default the file has the "py" extension. Always make sure your scripts are saved this way in order to be recognized as Python programs. Now if you run the program IDLE will open the interactive mode window and display the result.

For now, you've run your "Hello World" program by using IDLE. However, you normally want your applications to run like the ones you are currently using. This means you want an executable file which you double click and it runs. At the moment, if you click on the Python file a window will open and then abruptly close. You may be thinking that the program doesn't work because nothing happened, however something did happen. It was simply too fast for you to observe anything concrete. The program executed all of its instructions, which means that it displayed the message in a fraction of a second and then it terminated itself. What you need to do is keep the program running once it executes all of its commands so that you can see the results and interact with them. But before you do that, let's take a moment to discuss how to comment your code and make it readable and easy to understand.

Building Development environment;

An IDE, which stands for Integrated Development Environment, is a program designed with a number of features that are useful to programmers. It has a graphical interface and it makes typing code much faster due to autocomplete and history functions. Programming stays the same whether you are using a text editor or an IDE, however with the IDE you will benefit from many shortcuts, reminders, and error signaling and code autocorrect. Many IDE's even include suggestions on how to fix an error.

There are many IDE's to choose from, but one of the most popular ones is IDLE. It comes in the same package as Python, so there's no need to perform any extra steps. Keep in mind that it can run in two modes, namely interactive and script. Use interactive if you want Python to immediately respond to whatever commands you type.

Writing first python program

Open your script and type the following lines:

Hello World!

This is a demonstration of the "print" function.

If you run the program again, you will see that nothing changed. These lines you added aren't executed as code. They are known as comments and their purpose is to make the code of an application more understandable. You might be thinking that typing such information is a waste of time because as the programmer you already know what your code is about. That may be true, however when you write a complex program and then you abandon it for a week or two, you're going to have some trouble understanding the purpose of every function and variable. Sure, you can read your code and eventually figure everything out, but that is not a proper use of your time. Code comments are used to label and explain complicated functions so that you don't have to dive into the code itself. They are especially useful if another programmer is going to work on your program at a later date. Imagine a stranger having to decipher your personal approach to the development of your application. On a large project he could waste wakes of his time instead of doing some work in order to progress.

Comments are defined by the hash mark in front of a line. Each line you intend as a comment needs to have its own mark, otherwise you will get an error. If you're worried about the efficiency of your programs due to hundreds or even thousands of comments, you shouldn't be. They have no impact on your computer because when the code is executed, the machine ignores all comments and uses no additional resources.

Additionally, to make your comments and code more readable, you can leave empty lines. However, don't do this after every line of code. You use empty space in between blocks of code, or sections. Programs ignore blank space, so nothing will be affected by using it. Now let's get back to your first program. Add the following line after the print function:

input ("\n\n Hit the Enter key to exit!")

This line will display the console in which the line "Hello World!" is printed, and then display the line "Hit the Enter key to exit!" Finally, the program will stay open and wait for you until you hit the Enter key. This is a simple way to keep the program running until the user performs an action.

Chapter 3: What are Variables and Strings

A software application consists of two fundamental parts: Logic and Data. Logic consists of the functionalities that are applied on data to accomplish a particular task. Application data can be stored in memory or hard disk. Files and databases are used to store data on hard disk. In memory, data is stored in the form of variables. Definition of Variable

Variable in programming is a memory location used to store some value. Whenever you store a value in a variable, that value is actually being stored at physical location in memory. Variables can be thought of as reference to physical memory location. The size of the memory reserved for a variable depends upon the type of value stored in the variable.

Creating a Variable

It is very easy to create a variable in Python. The assignment operator "=" is used for this purpose. The value to the left of the assignment operator is the variable identifier or name of the variable. The value to the right of the operator is the value assigned to the variable. Take a look at the following code snippet.

Name = 'Mike' # A string variable

Age = 15 # An integer variable

Score = 102.5 # A floating type variable

Pass = True # A Boolean variable

In the script above we created four different types of variables. You can see that we did not specify the type of variable with the variable name. For instance we did not write "string Name" or "int Age". We only wrote the variable name. This is because Python is a loosely typed language. Depending upon the value being stored in a variable, Python assigns type to the variable at runtime. For instance when Python interpreter interprets the line "Age = 15", it checks the type of the value which is integer in this case. Hence, Python understands that Age is an integer type variable.

To check type of a variable, pass the variable name to "type" function as shown below: type(Age)

You will see that the above script, when run, prints "int" in the output which is basically the type of Age variables

Python allows multiple assignment which means that you can assign one value to multiple variables at the same time. Take a look at the following script:

Age = Number = Point = 20 #Multiple Assignment

print (Age)

print (Number)

print (Point)

In the script above, integer 20 is assigned to three variables: Age, Number and Point. If you print the value of these three variables, you will see 20 thrice in the output.

For any programming language, the basic part is to store the data in memory and process it. No matter what kind of operation we are going to perform, we must have the object of operation. It is difficult for a skillful woman to cook without rice. In Python language, constants and variables are the main ones. In fact, both of them are identification codes used by program designers to access data contents in memory.

The biggest difference between the two is that the contents of variables will change with the execution of the program, while the contents of constants are fixed forever. In the process of program execution, it is often necessary to store or use some data. For example, if you want to write a program to calculate the mid-term exam results, you must first input the students' results, and then output the total score, average score and ranking after calculation. This chapter describes how to store and access this data.

Variable Naming and Assignment

In a program, program statements or instructions tell the computer which Data to access and execute step by step according to the instructions in the program statements. These data may be words or numbers. What we call variable is the most basic role in a programming language, that is, a named memory unit allocated by the compiler in programming to store changeable data contents. The computer will store it in "memory" and take it out for use when necessary. In order to facilitate identification, it must be given a name. We call such an object "variable." For example:

> > firstsample = 3

> > > second sample = 5

> > > result = firstsample + secondsample

In the above program statement, firstsample, secondsample, result are variables, and number 3 is the variable value of firstsample. Since the capacity of memory is limited, in order to avoid wasting memory space, each variable will allocate memory space of different sizes according to requirements, so "Data Type" is used to regulate it.

Variable declaration and assignment

Python is an object-oriented language, all data are regarded as objects, and the method of an Object reference is also used in variable processing. The type of variable is determined when the initial value is given, so there is no need to declare the data type in advance. The value of a variable is assigned with "=" and beginners easily confuse the function of the assignment operator (=) with the function of "equal" in mathematics. In programming languages, the "=" sign is mainly used for assignment.

The syntax for declaring a variable is as follows:

variable name = variable value

e.g. number = 10.

The above expression indicates that the value 10 is assigned to the variable number. In short, in Python language, the data type does not need to be declared in advance when using a variable, which is different from that in C language, which must be declared in advance before using a variable. Python interpretation and operation system will automatically determine the data type of the variable according to the value of the variable given or set. For example, the data type of the above variable number is an integer. If the content of the variable is a string, the data type of the variable is a string.

Variable naming rules

For an excellent programmer, readability of program code is very important. Although variable names can be defined by themselves as long as they conform to Python's regulations, when there are more and more variables, simply taking variables with letter names such as abc will confuse people and greatly reduce readability. Considering the readability of the program, it is best to name it according to the functions and meanings given by variables. For example, the variable that stores height is named "Height" and the variable that stores weight is named "Weight." Especially when the program scale is larger, meaningful variable names will become more important. For example, when declaring variables, in order to make the program readable, it is generally used to start with lowercase letters, such as score, salary, etc. In Python, variable names also need to conform to certain rules. If inappropriate names are used, errors may occur during program execution. Python is a case-sensitive language. In other words, number and Number are two different variables. Variable names are not limited in length. Variable names have the following limitations: the first character of a variable name must be an English letter, underlined "_" and cannot be a number. Subsequent characters can match other upper- and lower-case English letters, numbers, underlined "_," and no space character is allowed. You cannot use Python's built-in reserved words (or keywords). Although Python version 3. X supports foreign language variable names; it is recommended that you try not to use words to name variables. On the one hand, it is more troublesome to switch input methods when inputting program code. On the other hand, the reading of program code will not be smooth. The so-called reserved word usually has special meaning and function, so it will be reserved in advance and cannot be used as a variable name or any other identifier name.

The following is an example of a valid variable name: pageresponse

fileName4563

level

Number_

dstance

The following is an example of an invalid variable name:

2_sample

for

$ levelone

The user name learning classroom uses the help () function to query Python reserved word. The help () function is Python's built-in function. If you are not sure about the method and property usage of a specific object, you can use the help () function to query.

The Python reserved words mentioned above can be viewed by using the help () function. As long as "help ()" is executed, the help interactive mode will be entered. In this mode, the instructions to be queried will be input, and the relevant instructions will be displayed.

We can continue to input the instructions we want to query in help mode. When we want to exit help interactive mode, we can input Q or quit. You can also take parameters when entering the help () command, such as help (" keywords "), Python will directly display help or description the information without entering help interactive mode.

Although Python uses dynamic data types, it is very strict in data processing, and its data type is "strong type." For example:

> > > firstsample = 5

> > > secondsample = "45"

> > > print (firstsample + secondsample) #

shows that TypeError variable firstsample is of numeric type and variable secondsample is of string type.

Some programming languages will convert the type unconsciously and automatically convert the value A to the string type, so firstsample + secondsample will get 545. Python language prohibits different data types from operating, so executing the above statement obviously Indicates information about the wrong type.

There is a difference between "strongly typed" and "weakly typed" in the data types of strong and weak type programming languages in small classrooms. One of the trade-offs is the safety of data type conversion.

The strong type has a strict inspection for data type conversion.

Different types of operations must be explicitly converted, and programs will not automatically convert. For example, Python and Ruby prefer strong types.

However, most weak type programming languages adopt Implicit Conversion. If you don't pay attention to it, unexpected type conversion will occur, which will lead to wrong execution results.

JavaScript is a weak type of programming language.

Static Type and Dynamic Type

When Python is executed, the way to determine the data type belongs to "dynamic type."

What is the dynamic type?

The data types of programming languages can be divided into "Statically-Typed" and "Dynamically-Typed" according to the type checking method.

1. **Static types** are compiled with the type checked first, so the variables must be explicitly declared

48

before they are used. The types of variables cannot be arbitrarily changed during execution. Java and C are such programming languages. For example, the following C language program statement declares that the variable number is of int integer type, and the initial value of the variable is set to 10. When we assign "apple" to number again, an error will occur, because "apple" is a string, and compilation will fail due to type discrepancy during compilation.

int firstsample = 10

firstsample = "apple"

#Error:

Types do not match

2. **Dynamic types** are compiled without prior type checking, and data types are determined according to variable values during execution. Therefore, there is no need to declare types before variables are used. The same variable can also be given different types of values, and Python is a dynamic type. For example, the

following program statement declares the variable number and sets the initial value to the integer 10. When we assign the string apple to number, the type will be automatically converted.

firstsample = 10

firstsample = "love"

Print (firstsample)

output string love

Python has a Garbage Collection mechanism. When the object is no longer in use, the interpreter will automatically recycle and free up memory space. In the above example, when the integer object number is reassigned to another string object, the original integer object will be deleted by the interpreter. If the object is determined not to be used, we can also delete it by using the "del" command with the following syntax: del object name

For example:

> > number = "apple"

> > > print(number) # output apple

> > > del number # deletes string object number

> > > print(number) #Error: number does not define the execution result.

Since the variable number has been deleted, if the number variable is used again, an undefined error message for the variable will appear.

Python Data Types

A programming application needs to store variety of data. Consider scenario of a banking application that needs to store customer information. For instance, a person's name and mobile number; whether he is a defaulter or not; collection of items that he/ she has loaned and so on. To store such variety of information, different data types are required. While you can create custom data types in the form of classes, Python provides six standard data types out of the box. They are:

Strings

Numbers

Booleans

Lists

Tuples

Dictionaries

Strings

Python treats string as sequence of characters. To create strings in Python, you can use single as well as double quotes. Take a look at the following script: first_name = 'mike' # String with single quotation last_name = " johns" # String with double quotation full_name = first_name + last_name # string concatenation using + print(full_name)

In the above script we created three string variables: first_name, last_name and full_name. String with single quotes is used to initialize the variable "first_name" while string with double quotes initializes the variable "last_name". The variable full_name contains the concatenation of the first_name and last_name variables. Running the above script returns following output: mike johns

Numbers

There are four types of numeric data in python:

int (Stores integer e.g 10)

float (Stores floating point numbers e.g 2.5)

long (Stores long integer such as 48646684333)

complex (Complex number such as 7j + 4847k)

To create a numeric Python variable, simply assign a number to variable. In the following script we create four different types of numeric objects and print them on the console. int_num = 10 # integer float_num = 156.2 #float long_num = -0.59774856134546 #long complex_num = -. 785 + 7J #Complex

print(int_num)

print(float_num)

print(long_num)

print(complex_num)

The output of the above script will be as follows:

Boolean

Boolean variables are used to store Boolean values. True and False are the two Boolean values in Python. Take a look at the following example:

defaulter = True

has_car = False

print(defaulter and has_car)

 In the script above we created two Boolean variables "defaulter" and "has_car" with values True and False respectively. We then print the result of the AND operation on both of these variables. Since the AND operation between True and False returns false, you will see false in the output.

Lists

In Python, List data type is used to store collection of values. Lists are similar to arrays in any other programming language. However Python lists can store values of different types. To create a list opening and closing square brackets are used. Each item in the list is separated from the other with a comma. Take a look at the following example.

```
cars = [' Honda', 'Toyota', 'Audi', 'Ford', 'Suzuki',
'Mercedez'] print( len( cars)) #finds total items in string
print( cars)
```

In the script above we created a list named cars. The list contains six string values i.e. car names. Next we printed the size of the list using len function. Finally we print the list on console.

Tuples

Tuples are similar to lists with two major differences. Firstly, opening and closing braces are used to create tuples instead of lists that use square brackets. Secondly, tuple once created is immutable which means that you cannot change tuple values once it is created. The following example clarifies this concept. cars = [' Honda', 'Toyota', 'Audi', 'Ford', 'Suzuki', 'Mercedez']

```
cars2 = (' Honda', 'Toyota', 'Audi', 'Ford', 'Suzuki',
'Mercedez')
```

```
cars [3] = 'WV'
```

```
cars2 [3] = 'WV'
```

In the above script we created a list named cars and a tuple named cars2. Both the list and tuple contains list of car names. We then try to update the third index of the list as well as tuple with a new value. The list will be updated but an error will be thrown while trying to update the tuple's third index. This is due to the fact that tuple, once created cannot be modified with new values.

Dictionaries

Dictionaries store collection of data in the form of key-value pairs. Each key-value pair is separated from the other via comma. Keys and values are separated from each other via colon. Dictionary items can be accessed via index as well as keys. To create dictionaries you need to add key-value pairs inside opening and closing parenthesis. Take a look at the following example.

cars = {' Name':' Audi', 'Model': 2008, 'Color':' Black'}

print(cars[' Color'])

print(cars.keys())

print(cars.values())

In the above script we created a dictionary named cars. The dictionary contains three key-value pairs i.e. 3 items. To access value, we can pass key to the brackets that follow dictionary name. Similarly we can use keys() and values() methods to retrieve all the keys and values from a dictionary, respectively.

Decimal Mode

This is a Python standard module library. Before using it, you need to import this module with import instruction before using it. After correctly importing this module, we can use the decimal. Decimal class to store accurate numbers. If the parameter is not an integer, we must pass in the parameter as a string.

For example:

import decimal

Num = decimal.decimal (" 0.1") + decimal.decimal (" 0.2")

And the result will be 0.3. Use the round () function to force the specified number of decimal places round(x[, n]) to be a built-in function, which returns the value closest to parameter x, and n is used to specify the number of decimal places returned.

For   example:
result = 0.1 + 0.2 The program statement above print (round(num, 1)) takes the variable num to one decimal place, thus obtaining a result of 0.3. 2.2.3 Boolean Data Type (bool) is a data type that represents the logic and is a subclass of int, with only True value (true) and False value (false). Boolean data types are commonly used in program flow control. We can also use the value "1" or "0" to represent true or false values. For example, the string and integer cannot be directly added, and the string must be converted to an integer. If all the operations are of numeric type, Python will automatically perform type conversion without specifying the forced conversion type.

For example:

num = 5 + 0.3

Result num = 5.3 (floating-point number)

Python will automatically convert an integer to floating-point number for operation. In addition, Boolean values can also be calculated as numeric values. True means 1, False means 0.

For example:

num = 5 + True

result num = 6 (integer).

If you want to convert strings to Boolean values, you can convert them by bool function. Use the print () function in the following sample program to display

Boolean values.

[sample procedure: bool.py] converts bool type

print(bool(0))

print(bool(""))

 print(bool(" "))

print(bool(1))

The execution results of the 05

print(bool(" ABC ") sample

program are shown. Program Code Resolution: Line 02: An empty string was passed in, so False was returned. Line 03 returns True because a string containing a space is passed in. When using Boolean, it values False and True, pay special attention to the capitalization of the first letter.

Constant

Constant refers to the value that the program cannot be changed during the whole execution process. For example, integer constants: 45, -36, 10005, 0, etc., or floating-point constants: 0.56, -0.003, 1.234E2, etc. Constants have fixed data types and values. The biggest difference between variable and constant is that the content of the variable changes with the execution of the program, while the constant is fixed. Python's constant refers to the literal constant, which is the literal meaning of the constant. For example, 12 represents the integer 12. The literal constant is the value written directly into the Python program. If literal constants are distinguished by data type, there will be different classifications, for example, 1234, 65, 963, and 0 are integer literal constants. The decimal value is the literal constant of the floating-point types, such as 3.14, 0.8467, and 744.084. As for the characters enclosed by single quotation marks (') or double quotation marks ("), they are all string literal constants. For example," Hello World "and" 0932545212 "are all string literal constants.

Formatting Input and Output Function

In the early stage of learning Python, the program execution results are usually output from the control panel or the data input by the user is obtained from the console. Before, we often use the print () function to output the program's execution results. This section will look at how to call the print () function for print format and how to call the input () function to input data.

The print format

The print () function supports the print format. There are two formatting methods that can be used, one is print format in the form of "%" and the other is print format in the form function. "%" print format formatted text can use "% s" to represent a string, "% d" to represent an integer, and "% f" to represent a floating-point number.

The syntax is as follows:

PRINT (formatted text (parameter 1, parameter 2, ..., parameter n)) For example:

score = 66 Print (" History Score: %d"% score")

Output

Result: History Score: 66 %d is formatted, representing the output integer format. The print format can be used to control the position of the printout so that the output data can be arranged in order.

For example:

print("% 5s history result: %5.2f"% (" Ram," 95)) The output results of the sample program print("% 5s history results: %5.2f"% (" Raj," 80.2))

The formatted text in the above example has two parameters, so the parameters must be enclosed in brackets, where %5s indicates the position of 5 characters when outputting, and when the actual output is less than 5 characters, a space character will be added to the left of the string. %5.2f represents a floating-point number with 5 digits output, and the decimal point occupies 2 digits. The following example program outputs the number 100 in floating-point number, octal number, hexadecimal number and binary number format using the print function, respectively.

You can practice with this example program:

[Example Procedure:

print_%. py]

Integer Output

visual = 100 in Different Decimal Numbers

print (" floating point number of number %s: %5.1f"% (visual, visual))

\print (" octal of number %s: %o"% (visual, visual))
print (" hex of number %s: %x"% (visual, visual))

The execution result of the print (" binary of number %s: %s"% (visual, bin(visual))) will be displayed.

Program code analysis:

Lines 02-04: output in the format of floating-point number octal number and hexadecimal number. Line 05: Since binary numbers do not have formatting symbols, decimal numbers can be converted into binary characters through the built-in function bin () and then output.

The output

Print format of the format () function can also be matched with the format () function. Compared with the% formatting method, the format () function is more flexible. Its usage is as follows: print("{} is a hard-working student ... ." format (" First ranker ")). Generally, the simple FORMAT usage will be replaced by the braces "{}," which means that the parameters in FORMAT () are used within {}. The format () function is quite flexible and has two major advantages: regardless of the parameter data type, it is always indicated by {}. Multiple parameters can be used, the same parameter can be output multiple times, and the positions can be different.

For example: print("{ 0} this year is {1} years old ... ." format (" First ranker ," 18)), where {0} means to use the first parameter, {1} means to use the second parameter, and so on. If the number inside {} is omitted, it will be filled in sequentially.

We can also use the parameter name to replace the corresponding parameter,

for example: print("{ name} this year {age}.." format(name =" First ranker ," age = 18)) can specify the output format of the parameter by adding a colon":" directly after the number. For example: print('{ 0:. 2f}'. format(5.5625)) means the first parameter takes 2 decimal places. In addition, the string can be centered, left-aligned, or right-aligned with the "<" ">" symbol plus the field width.

For example:

 print("{ 0: 10} score: {1: _ 10}." format (" Ram," 95))
print("{ 0: 10} results: {1: > 10}." format(" Raj," 87))

The output of the print("{ 0: 10} result: {1:* < 10}." format(" Ram," 100)) program is shown. {1: _ 10} indicates that the output field width is 10, and the following line "_" is filled and centered. {1: > 10} indicates that the output field is 10 wide and aligned to

65

the right, and the unspecified padding characters will be filled with spaces. {1:* < 10} indicates that the output field is 10 wide, filled with an asterisk "*" and aligned to the left.

Input Function:

Input() input is a common input instruction, which allows users to input data from "standard input device" (usually refers to keyboard) and transfer the numerical value, character or string entered by users to the specified variable. For example, if you calculate the total score of history and mathematics for each student, you can use the input command to let the user input the results of Chinese and mathematics, and then calculate the total score.

The syntax is as follows:

variable = input (prompt string) when data is Entered, and the enter key is pressed, the entered data will be assigned to the variable. The "prompt string" in the above syntax is a prompt message informing the user to enter, for example, the user is expected to enter height, and the program then outputs the value of height.

The program code is as follows:

height = input (" Give exact your height:")

For example, score = input (" Give exact your math score:")

The output of the print("% s' math score: %5.2f"% (" ram," float(score))) When the program is executed, it will wait for the user to input data first when it encounters the input instruction. After the user completes the input and presses the Enter key, it will store the data input by the user into the variable score. The data input by the user is in string format. We can convert the input string into an integer, floating-point number, and bool type through built-in functions such as int (), float (), bool (). The format specified in the example is floating point number (% 5.2f), so call float () function to convert the input score value into floating point number. The next section will introduce more complete data type conversion. If we use an integrated development environment such as Spyder, don't forget to switch the input cursor to Python console before inputting when the program is executed to input prompt information. Let's practice the use of input and output again through the sample program.

[Example Procedure: Format. Py] format.py】

name = input (" Give exact Name:")

che_grade = input (" Give a language score:")

math_grade = input (" Give Math Score:")

print("{ 0: 10} {1: > 6} {2: > 5}."

format (" name," "language," "mathematics"))

The execution results of the 06print ("{ 0: < 10} {1: > 5} {2: > 7}." format (name, che _ grade, math _ grade)).

Program Code Analysis:

Lines 01-03: Require users to enter their names, Chinese scores, and math scores in sequence.

Lines 05 and 06: output the names, Chinese and math headers in sequence, and then output the names and results of the two subjects in the next line.

Data type conversion requires operations between different types in expressions. We can convert data types "temporarily," that is, data types must be forced to be converted.

There are three built-in functions in Python that cast data types.

1. int ():

Cast to integer data type For example: x = "5" num = 5 + int(x) Print(dude) # Result: The value of 10 variable x is "5" and is of string type, so int(x) is called first to convert to integer type.

2. float ():

Cast to floating point data type

For example: x = "5.3"

dude = 5 + float(x)

Print(dude) # Result: The value of 10.3 variable X is "5.3" and is of string type, so float(x) is first used to convert to floating point type.

3. str ():

Cast to string data type

For example: first = "5.3"

dude = 5 + float(first)

Print (" The output value is" + str(dude)) # Result: The output value is 10.3.

In the above program statement, the string of words "the output value is" in the print () function is a string type, the "+" sign can add two strings, and the variable dude is a floating point type, so the str () function must be called first to convert it into a string. [sample procedure: conversion.py]

data type conversion

str = "{ 1} +{ 0} = {2}"

first = 150

second = "60"

The execution result of 04 print(str.format(first, second, first + int(second))) program

Line 01:

Since B is a string, specify its display format first. Note that the numerical numbering sequence of braces' {}' is {1}, {0}, {2}, so the display sequence of variables A and B is different from the parameter sequence in Format. Line 04:

First, call int () to convert b to an integer type, and then calculate.

Practice Exercise

-The pocket money bookkeeping butler designed a Python program that can input the pocket money spent seven days a week and output the pocket money spent every day. The sample program illustrates that this program requires the user name to be entered, and then the sum of spending for each day of the week can be entered continuously, and the pocket money spent for each day can be output. Program code shows that the following is the complete program code of this example program. [example program: money.py] pocket money bookkeeping assistant # -*- coding: utf-8 -*- """ You can enter pocket money spent 7 days a week and output the pocket money spent every day. """ name = value (" Give name:")

working1 = value (" Give the total amount of pocket money for the first working:")

working2 = value (" Give the total amount of pocket money for the next working:")

working3 = value (" Give the total amount of pocket money for the third working:")

working4 = value (" Give the total amount of pocket money for the fourth working:")

working5 = value (" Give the total spending of pocket money for the fifth working:")

working6 = value (" Give the total spending of pocket money for the sixth working:")

working7 = input (" Give the total allowance for the seventh working:")

```
print("{ 0: < 8}{ 1: ^ 5}{ 2: ^ 5}{ 3: ^ 5}{ 4: ^ 5}{
5: ^ 5}{ 6: ^ 5}{ 7: ^ 5}." \

format(" name,"" working1,"" working2,"" working3," \
"working4,""  working5,""  working6,"  \  "working7"))
print("{ 0: < 8}{ 1: ^ 5}{ 2: ^ 5}{ 3: ^ 5}{ 4: ^ 5}{
5: ^ 5}{ 6: ^ 5}{ 7: ^ 5}." \ format( name, working1,
working2,  working3,  working4,  working5,  working6,
working7))
```

Chapter 4: Operators in Python

You will realize that some program requests specific information or show the text on the screen. Sometimes we start the program code by informing the readers about our programs. To make things look easy for the other coders, it is important to give it the name or title that is simple and descriptive.

As a programmer, you can use a string literal that comprises the print function to get the right data. String literal is a line of the text surrounded by the quotes. They can be either double or single quotes. Although the type of quotes a programmer use matters less, the programmer must end with the quotes that he/she has used at the beginning of the phrase. You can command your computer to display a phrase or a word on the screen by just doing as discussed above.

Files

Apart from using the print function to obtain a string when printing on the screen, it can be used to write something onto the file. First, you will have to open up the myfile.txt and write on it before assigning it the

74

myfile which is a variable. Once you have completed the first step, you will have to assign "w" in the new line to tell the program that you will only write or make changes after the file has opened. It is not mandatory to use print function; just use the right methods like read method.

Read method is used to open specific files to help you read the available data. You can use this option to open a specific file. Generally, the read method helps the programmers to read the contents into variable data, making it easy for them to open the program they would like to read.

<u>Integers</u>

Always make sure that the integers are kept as whole numbers if you are using them. They can be negative or positive only if there are no decimals. However, if your number has a decimal point, use it as a floating number. Python will automatically display such integers in the screen.

Moreover, you cannot place one number next to others if you are using the integers because Python is a strongly typed language; thus it will not recognize them when you use them together. However, you put both the number and the string together by making sure you turn the number into a string first before going to the next steps.

TRIPLE QUOTES

After reading and understanding both the single and double quotes, it is now a time to look at the triple quotes. The triple quotes are used to define the literal that spans many lines. You can use three singles, double, or single when defining an authentic.

<u>Strings</u>

Although a string is seen as a complicated thing to many beginners, it is a term used by the programmers when referring to a sequence of characters and works just like a list. A string contains more functionality which is specific than a list. You will find it challenging to format the strings when writing out the code because some messages will not be fixed easily due to its functionality. String formatting is the only way to go away within such a situation.

ESCAPE SEQUENCES

They are used to donate special characters which are hard to type on the keyboard or those that can be reserved to avoid confusion that may occur in programming.

OPERATOR PRECEDENCE

It will help you to track what you are doing in Python. In fact, it makes things easy when ordering the operation to receive the right information. So, take enough time to understand how the operator precedence works to avoid confusion.

Variables

Variables refer to the labels donated somewhere in the computer memory to store something like holding values and numbers. In the programming typed statistically, the variables have predetermined values. However, Python enables you to use one variable to store many different types. For example, in the calculator, variables are like memory function to hold values which can be retrieved in case you need them later. The variables can only be erased if you store them in the newer value. You will have to name the variable and ensure it has an integer value.

Moreover, the programmer can define a variable in Python by providing the label value. For instance, a programmer can name a variable count and even make it an integer of one, and this can be written as; count=1. It allows you to assign the same name to the variable, and in fact, the Python interpreter cannot read through the information if you are trying to access values in the undefined variable. It will display a message showing syntax error. Also, Python provides you with the opportunity of defining different variables in one line even though this not a good according to our experience.

THE SCOPE OF A VARIABLE

It is not easy to access everything in Python, and there will be differences in the length of the variables. However, the way we define the variable plays a vital role in determining the location and the duration of accessing the variables. The part of the program that allows you to access the variable is called the Scope while the time taken for accessing the variable is a lifetime.

Global variables refer to the variables defined in the primary file body. These variables are visible throughout the file and also in the file that imports specific data. As such, these variables cause a long-term impact which you may notice when working on your program. This is the reason why it is not good to use global variables in the Python program. We advise programmers to add stuff into the global namespace only if they plan to use them internationally. A local variable is a variable defined within another variable. You can access local variables from the region they are assigned. Also, the variables are available in the specific parts of the program.

MODIFYING VALUES

For many programming languages, it is easy for an individual to define a particular variable whose values have been set. The values which cannot be modified or changed, in the programming language, are called constants. Although this kind of restrictions is not allowed in Python, there are used to ensure some variables are marked indicating that no one should change those values. You must write the name in capital letters, separated with underscores. A good example is shown below.

NUMBER_OF_HOURS_IN_A_DAY=24

It is not mandatory to put the correct number at the end. Since Python programming does not keep tracking and has no rules for inserting the correct value at the end, you are free and allowed to say, for example, that they are 25 hours in a day. However, it is important to put the correct value for other coders to use in case they want.

Modifying values is essential in your string as it allows a programmer to change the maximum number in the future. Therefore, understanding the working of the string in the program contributes a lot to the success of your program. One has to learn and know where to store the values, the rules governing each value, and how to make them perform well in a specific area.

THE ASSIGNMENT OPERATOR

Although discussed in this book earlier, we had not given it the specific name. It refers to an equal sign (=). You will be using the assignment operator to assign values to the variable located at the left side on the right of the statement. However, you must evaluate if the value on the right side is an arithmetic expression. Note that the assignment operator is not a mathematical sign in the programming because, in programming, we are allowed to add all types of things and make them look like they are equivalent to a certain number. This sign is used to show that those items can be changed or turned into the part on the other side.

Chapter 5: Conditional and loops in Python

Escape Sequences

Single and Double Quotes

Example

Start IDLE.

Navigate to the File menu and click New Window.

Type the following:


```
print('They said, "We need a new team?"')# escape with single quotes
```

```
# escaping double quotes
```

```
    print("They said, \" We  need a new team\"")
```

Escape Sequences in Python

The escape sequences enable us to format our output to enhance clarity to the human user. A program will still run successful without using escape sequences but the output will be highly confusing to the human user. Writing and displaying output in expected output is part of good programming practices. The following are commonly used escape sequences.

Method	Description	Method	Description
\n	ASCII Linefeed	\b	ASCII Backspace
\"	Double quote	\\	Backslash.
\f	ASCII Formfeed	\a	ASCII Bell
\newline	Backslash and newline ignored	\'	Single quote
\r	ASCII Carriage Return	\t	ASCII Horizontal Tab
\v	ASCII Vertical Tab	\ooo	Character with octal value ooo
\xHH	Character with hexadecimal value HH		

Examples

Start IDLE.

Navigate to the File menu and click New Window.

Type the following:

```
print("D:\\Lessons\\Programming")

print("Prints\n in two lines")
```

83

if....else conditional statement

We are going to take a look at the most basic form, and then we will work our way up from there. This is the easiest method to help you get a feel for how these 'if' statements are supposed to work. With this option, your program is only going to proceed if the user puts in the right answer and the program will refuse to proceed if you put in the wrong answer. There are a few limitations to putting this one to use, but it is better to get started one way or another, and this can be used as a foundation.

Let's look at how this code is working. There are a couple of things that you should see happening with this code. If the user is in our program and they state that they are 18 years old or younger, the program will continue to work as a result. Those people who don't enter the correct information will, for example, see this message instead: "You are not eligible for voting, try next election!" When the user sees this message appear on the screen, this will be the end of the small program that we just wrote, but you can certainly add some more to it later on. With this code, if the user ends up putting in an age that is over 18, the program is not going to provide them with a result. Their age is not wrong, but it doesn't match the conditions that you set, so it doesn't have anything to send over at this point.

With this particular program, if the user tells the computer that they are 25 years old, the program is set up to tell that this age does not meet the conditions that you set. Because the conditions have not been met at this point, the 'if' statement that we used is going to end the program right now. This can have some limitations because you do not want the code to just randomly stop right here, but that is what will happen based on what was placed in your code.

As we have mentioned, there will be times that you just want the code to respond no matter what answer the user provides. You want the user to put in that they are 25 or some other age without having the program shut down on them. The first statements that we looked at were the 'if' statements, but to get the program to respond regardless of what kind answer is put in, you will want to work with the 'if else' statements.

With the 'if else' statement, it will not matter what the user puts into the program. If the conditions you set out are not met, the program will simply move on to the second part and decide to implement what you placed in there.

As you can imagine, this is an option that will open up a lot more possibilities to what you can do compared to the 'if' statement that we worked on before. You will have two options that you can use with this one so that something will always show up on the screen. Later we will even learn how to take more than two answers to make the program work.

With the additional option that comes up, the user will be able to put in any age that you will like. If the user types in that they are 17, for example, the statement about them being too young to vote will show up on the screen. But if they put in an age that is over 18, they will get the second statement to show up instead.

You will find that there is a lot more freedom to creating a useful code when you work with the 'if else' statements. You are able to add in three, four, and even more options so that a specific message will show up based on how you want your code to work. The 'if else' statements can be used to make it easier for you to get the program to react and to what your user is doing, no matter which answers they decide to place inside.

Now, the example above of the if...else statements is pretty simple, and it is possible for you to go through and add in more steps to the code as well. For example, if you want to allow the user to put in more than two answers, such as three or four options, you can do this just by adding in more parts to the code. You could choose to have a different message come up for those who are in the 16 to 18 age group, one that is for those who are 19 to 25 years old, and another for those who are at least 26 years old. There are a lot of possibilities and methods that you can use, you just need to look at the program that you want to work with and then split it all up based on what will work the best for your code.

How to work with 'elif' statements

There is a third 'if' statement that you could work with as well. This one is known as the 'elif' statement. We spent some time earlier in this guidebook looking at the basics of the 'if' statements and how they are different compared to the 'if else' statements. Both of these are great for adding in a sense of interaction to your code. These allow the user to pick out from some options or to add in their own information and the code will be able to interact with the user without trouble. The elif statements can help take this to the next level to deliver great results.

The elif statements are simple enough to use and easy to learn. Not to mention, you can also add in more of these statements to your code as much as you would like. The example that we will show in a bit will give the user three different options to choose from as well as a catch-all that the user can go with if they are not happy with any of the other answers. This is just to keep things simple. You can add as many of these 'elif' statements as you would like which also means you can add in as many of these statements as you need to make the code work. That is one of the great things about working with the elif statements; it gives you a lot of freedom to make sure the code works for you. Now that you know a little bit more about what the elif statement is all about, it is time to take a look at an example so that you can see this one working.

Remember that the option below is just a simple elif statement and you can certainly add more to it to get the results that you want from the code.

When you place this into your compiler, it is going to come up on the screen so that the user is able to choose from the choices that you have listed. The user can easily pick out the number that goes with the pizza of their choice. There is also an option for you to go with in case the user doesn't want any of the pizzas and they would like to get a drink instead. This is known as the 'elif' statement and is meant to catch on to all of the options that the user wants but are not listed above.

And that is how the 'if' statements work. You can set up the conditions that you want to work with so that the program behaves exactly as planned. You can make it so that there is only one right answer, make it so that the user is able to input any answer that they want and a variety of answers will show up, or you can make a menu list so that the user can pick any item what they want. This allows the user to have a ton of interaction with your program.

Loops

There is nothing worse than having to repeat the same task multiple times. For this reason, most people choose to count sheep if they are unable to fall asleep. This has nothing to do with the fact that woolly mammals can help put you to sleep. People only do this because they find it easier to fall asleep when they have to repeat a boring task. Their mind usually shuts off and they go to sleep since they are not performing an interesting task.

Using Loops

If you want to print the word hello five times, you can enter the following code:

```
>>> print("hello")

hello

>>> print("hello")

hello

>>> print("hello")

hello
```

```
>>> print("hello")

hello

>>> print("hello")

hello
```

This is, however, a tedious process. There is a better way to do this, and that is to use the loop to reduce the number of times you write the same code.

```
>>> for x in range(0, 5):

print('hello')

hello

hello

hello

hello

hello
```

The range function in the first line of the code will help you create a list of numbers that begin from the starting number until the number right before the ending one. This may seem a little confusing; so let us break it down. Let us first combine the range and list functions and see how the combination works. The range function will not create the list of numbers, but will return an iterator. This iterator is an object found in Python that was designed specifically for loops. If you combine the range function with the list function, you will obtain a list of numbers.

```
>>> print(list(range(10, 20)))
```

[10, 11, 12, 13, 14, 15, 16, 17, 18, 19]

In the case of the program with the for loop, the first line of code is telling Python to perform the following functions:

- **Assign the value zero to the iterator and begin counting from zero until the value of the iterator is 5.**

- **Store the value of the iterator in the variable x in every iteration.**

Python will then execute the block of code after the loop. When you enter the code in IDLE, it will automatically be indented. When you hit enter after you type the second line, Python will print the string five times.

Alternatively, the variable x can also be used to count the number of times the string is being printed.

```
>>> for x in range(0, 5):
print('hello %s' % x)
hello 0
hello 1
hello 2
hello 3
hello 4
```

If you choose to get rid of the for loop one more time, the code will look like this:

```
>>> x = 0
>>> print('hello %s' % x)
hello 0
>>> x = 1
>>> print('hello %s' % x)
hello 1
```

```
>>> x = 2

>>> print('hello %s' % x)

hello 2

>>> x = 3

>>> print('hello %s' % x)

hello 3

>>> x = 4

>>> print('hello %s' % x)

hello 4
```

When you use the loop, you will not have to write so many lines of code. Most programmers hate performing the same action multiple times; that's why they prefer to use the **for loop**. This is one of the most popular statements used in every programming language. It is important to remember that you do not have to stick to the range when you use a for loop.

In the first line of code, we are trying to create a list that will contain the items 'huge', 'hairy', and 'pants.' In the second line of code, we are trying to loop through these items. When Python loops through the list, it will assign one item to the iterator variable 'i' in every iteration. The contents of the list are then being printed on the screen using the next two lines of code. When you press **Enter**, the next line of code will tell Python that it should end the code, and run the next block where it will print the items in the list twice. You should remember that if you enter the incorrect number of spaces in the code Python will display an indentation error.

In the previous chapter, you learned that it is important to maintain the indentation in Python to avoid any errors. You can insert any number of spaces before you write the code, but you must ensure that the number of spaces is consistent across every line in the code.

Python will enter the first loop and print the items that are present in the list in the first line of the code. It will then enter the next loop and print the items that are present in the next list. It will continue with the print(i) command for the items in the list, followed by the complete list using the command print(j). Let us look at something a little more practical and not just print some silly words on the screen. If you remember the calculation that we performed in the third chapter, we calculated the number of coins that you will have at the end of the year after you duplicated the gold coins using your grandmother's invention. The equation looked like this:

>>> 20 + 10 * 365 – 3 * 52

The equation represents the 20 coins that you have found and the 10 coins that your grandmother's invention has spat out. Ten is multiplied by 365. The equation also accounts for the three coins that the raven steals every week.

It is always a good idea to see how the number of gold coins you own will increase every week. You can do this by using another for loop, but before that, you will need to change the value of the variable magic_coins. This variable should now represent the number of magic coins that you will have at the end of every week.

While We Continue to Talk About Loops

A for loop isn't the only kind of loop you can make in Python. There's also the while loop. The former is of a specific length, whereas the latter is used when you don't know ahead of time when it needs to stop looping. Imagine a staircase with 20 steps.

Let us look at the following example. There is a staircase that has been built on the side of a tall mountain. You will run out of energy before you reach the top of the mountain. There is a possibility that the weather will become bad, which will make you stop. You can put this example into a while loop in the following manner:

step = 0

while step < 10000:

print(step)

if tired == True:

break

elif badweather == True:

```
break

else:

step = step + 1
```

If you try to enter and run this code, you'll get an error. Why? The error happens because we haven't created the variables tired and badweather. Although there isn't enough code here to actually make a working program, it does demonstrate a basic example of a while loop. We start by creating a variable called step with step = 0. Next, we create a while loop that checks whether the value of the variable step is less than 10,000 (step < 10000), which is the total number of steps from the bottom of the mountain to the top. As long as step is less than 10,000, Python will execute the rest of the code.

So, the steps of a while loop are as follows:

1. Check out the condition.

2. Implement the code in the block.

3. Repeat.

Do you know how this loop will work? We begin counting the variable at 45, and this number is assigned to the variable x, and at 80 is assigned to the variable y. When the code in the loop is run, the value for both variables x and y will increase. The loop will continue to run until the condition holds true. Since the value of the variable x will reach 50 in the fifth iteration, the condition does not hold true. Python will then stop running the statements in the block of code.

You can also use the while loop to create a semi-eternal loop. This type of a loop will go on forever unless there is something that will make Python come out of the loop. This means that Python will need to break out of the loop. Let us look at the following example:

while True:

lots of code here

lots of code here

lots of code here

if

some_value == True:

break

Since the condition used in the while loop is always true, the statements in the block of code will always run. This means that the loop will run endlessly. Python will come out of the loop if the variable some_value holds the value True.

Chapter 6: Modules and Functions in Python

Explain functions in python;

Python Functions and Modules

Module

Modules in Python are going to enable you to organize your Python code in a manner that makes sense.

Whenever code is grouped together that is similar, then it is going to make the code not only easier to understand, but the code is also going to be more user friendly.

The objects in a module are going to be named after things that you are going to be able to bind and reference at a later date.

An easier way to think of it is that modules are similar to files that are full of Python code. The module will ultimately define a variable, function, or class.

Modules are also runnable code.

Example

Def print_func (par) :

Print "Good bye : " , par

Return

Import statements

The source files in Python can be used as a module if you import the statement into another source file.

Syntax

Import module1 [, module 2 [, ... moduleA]

Python's interpreter is going to import the module but only if it has a path to follow.

The search path's are going to be a directory list where the interpreter will search to find the correct module before it is imported.

Example

#!/usr/bin/python

#import help for module

Import help

#At this point the function can be defined

Help.print_func ("Tim")

Output

Good bye : Tim

You can import a module as many times as you want, but it is not going to change the fact that it is only going to be loaded into the script once.

This was put into place by the creators of Python so that the execution of the module does not happen each time that it is imported.

From...Import

A from statement in Python ensures that you can bring the attributes that you want into the module from where it is stored.

Syntax

From modname import name1 [, name 2[, ... nameB]]

Example

From dig import dignity

This statement is not going to import the entire module, but it is going to bring the module into the script.

Names can also be imported from the modules that are in your directory by using a slightly different syntax.

From modname import *

This syntax makes it easy for all of the module to be imported into this space, but, this function should be used sparingly.

Module location

After a module has been imported into the code of Python, it is going to be searched for in a very specific order so that Python can ensure that it is getting the correct module.

First it is going to search the directory that you are currently in.

Next it is going to go through all the directories that are inside of PYTHONPATH

Lastly, it is going to check the UNIX directory which is going to be the default path.

The search path is going to be inside of the module under the variable of sys.path.

This variable is going to be in one of the three directories mentioned above.

PYTHONPATH

As an environment variable, PYTHONPATH is going to be able to show all of the directories that are inside of Python.

Calling a function in python;

A function that has been defined will only set the parameters for it and then give it its name.

At the point in time that you have set the structure for the block of code, you are going to be able to execute it by creating another function or by using Python directly in a prompt that is provided by the program.

Example

```
#! / usr/ bin/ python
```

#the definition for my function is going to entered in here

Def printme (str) :

"This will be where the string is printed"

Print str

Return;

at this point I am going to be able to call upon the printme function

Printme ("This will be where the first definition is going to go")

Printme ("This is the second definition")

Output

This will be where the first definition is going to go.

This is the second definition.

Value vs Pass by reference

When a parameter is set in Python, it has to be passed by a reference.

This means that if you are wanting to change the parameter, any change that you end up making is going to be reflected back to the function that has been called.

Example

```
#!/ usr/ bin/ python

#define your function in this space

Def nameme ( asection ) :

"This is going to be before you change anything"

Asection. Append ( [ 5, 10, 15, 20 ] );

Print "the numbers in the function I created: " , asection

Return

#here is where you are going to change your function

Asection = [ 2, 4, 6 ];

Nameme( asection ) ;

Print "Any number that is not in the function " , asection

Output

Numbers in the function [ 2, 4, 6, [ 5, 10, 15, 20 ] ]
```

Numbers not in the function [2, 4, 6, [5, 10, 15, 20]]

Argument functions

There are four types of arguments that are going to be used with functions

Variable-length arguments

Required arguments

Default arguments

Keyword arguments

Required

Arguments are going to be sent through the function in the order in which the arguments are in order. It is known as a required argument.

There are various other arguments that can be used, however, the argument that you pick needs to match the definition of the function exactly or you are going to end up with an error from Python.

When you are calling upon a function, you have to ensure that it passes at least one argument or else you will end up with a error that is syntax based.

Example

```
#!/ usr/ bin / python

#definition of the function belongs here

Def nameme ( str )
```

"This will be the string that is written inside of the function"

```
Print str

Return ;

#this will be where the function is called upon

Nameme( )
```

Because no argument has been listed, you are going to end up receiving an error and having to go back and fix your code.

Keyword

Keyword arguments are going to function like when a function is called upon.

The keyword argument is going to be defined by the name of the parameter.

Thanks to this argument, you are going to be able to skip arguments or put them in a different order since the interpreter is going to be able to look at the keywords and then match it with the parameter that it needs to be placed with.

Example

#!/ usr/ bin / python

#definition of the function

Def nameme (str) :

"The string is going to be printed here"

Print str

Return ;

#the function can now be called upon here

Nameme (str – "A section ")

Output

A section

As previously stated, you are going to be able to put your parameters where you want them without worrying about getting an error message.

Example

```
#! / usr/ bin / python

#definition of the function belongs here

Def printdata ( title, years of service ) :

"The data that is put into the function has to be passed through this"

Print "title: " , title

Print "years of service " , years of service

Return ;

#the function can now be called upon

Printdata ( years of service = 5, title = associate
```

Output

Title: associate

Years of service: 5

Defaults

Values that are not given inside of the function are going to fall back on a value that Python has deemed the default value.

Example

```
#!/ usr / bin / python

#define your function in this section

Def printdata ( title, years of service = 5) :

"The data has to be passed through this function"

Print "title : " , title

Print "years of service " , years of service

Return ;

#here is where the function will be called

Printdata ( years of service = 15, title = "associate" )

Printdata ( title = "associate" )
```

Output

Title: associate

Years of service 5

Title: associate

Years of service 15

Docstrings;

It is placed after the function header as the first statement and explains in summary what the function does. Docstring should always be placed between triple quotes to accommodate multiple line strings.

Calling/Invoking the docstring we typed earlier

Example

Start IDLE.

Navigate to the File menu and click New Window.

Type the following:

print(welcome._doc_)

The output will be "This function welcomes you to

the individual passed in as

parameter".

The syntax for calling/invoking the docstring is:

print(function_name. _doc_)

Variable length arguments are going to have no name and they are not going to be like the default and required arguments.

Variable length arguments are going to be used whenever more arguments need to be used but you did not put in enough arguments when you were creating your function.

Syntax

Def functionname ([formal_ args,] *var_args_tuple) :

"function_docstring"

Function_suite

Return [expression]

The asterisks is going to take the place of any value that is used in the variable arguments that do not have keywords.

Should no other arguments be found, then the tuple that is in the function is going to remain empty.

Example

#! / usr/ bin/ python

#place the definition here

Def printdata (par1 , *tuple variable) :

"The argument will be printed here"

Print "the result will be : "

Print par1

For var in tuple variable :

Print var

Return ;

#the function will be called from here

Printdata (25)

Printdata (60, 98, 100)

Output

10

Output

60

98

100

Anonymous Functions

Functions that fall under this heading are not going to be placed in the directory in the manner in which other functions are.

Anonymous functions will use the keyword def.

Should you want to make smaller anonymous functions, you can use the keyword lambda.

These forms are going to be able to handle any number of arguments that you put into it. But, you are only going to get a single value returned inside of the expression. There are not going to be any commands and it cannot handle multiple expressions.

Lambda functions are not like inline statements

Anonymous functions are not able to have a call that is direct for it to print since lambda is going to require that you enter an expression.

These functions are going to have their own namespace on the local directory. Variables are not going to be accessed unless they are in the list for the parameter.

Syntax

Lambda [arg1 [, arg2, …. Argn]] : expression

Example

#!/ usr/bin/python

#definition of the function

Addition = lambda par1, par2: par1 + par2 ;

#the addition that you did is not going to be placed in the function

Print "sum of total : " , sum (15, 65)

Print "sum of total : " , sum (5, 80)

Output

Sum of total: 80

Sum of total : 85

Returned statements

These statements are going to leave the function and may or may not go back through the expression as they go back to the caller.

Returned statements that are not going to have any arguments will end up being returned as none.

Example

#! / usr/ bin/ python

the function will be defined here

```
Def addition ( par1 , par2 ) :

#add both of the parameters together

Sum = par1 + par2

Print "sum inside of the function : " , sum

Return sum ;

#the function is now going to be called upon

Sum = addition ( 15, 25 ) ;

Print "variables that fall outside of the function : " , sum
```

Output

Variables in the function : 40

Variables outside of the function : 40

Variable scopes

It will depend on where you are going to be in the program to depend on if you are going to have access to the variable that you want or not.

A variable's scope is going to be the determining factor for if the part of the program where you are is going to have the reach to get the identifier that you are wanting.

There are two scopes in Python

Global variables

Local variables

Local vs Global

When a variable is inside of the function, it is going to be known as a local variable. If it is found outside of the function, then it is a global variable.

Local variables can only be accessed when you are working inside of the function, but you have to make sure that they are declared first.

Global functions can be accessed at any point in the program.

You need to declare variables in the functions so that the scope is in the proper place.

Example

```
#! / usr/bin/python

Sum = 2; #this will be the global variable

#define your function in this slot

Def total ( par1, par 2 ) :

        #both arguments need to be added together

        Sum = par1 + par2 ; #the total is going to
    be a local variable

        Print "the function inside of the total for the
    local variable : " , sum

        Return total ;

#this will be where the function is called

Sum ( 5, 1 ) ;

Print "the total for the global functions : " , sum

Output

Inside: 6

Outside: 0
```

Python function return statement;

return [list of expressions]

Discussion

The return statement can return a value or a None object.

Example

Print(welcome("Richard"))   #Passing arguments and calling the function

Welcome Richard. Lovely Day!

None   #the returned value

Start IDLE.

Navigate to the File menu and click New Window.

Type the following:

```python
def my_function (balling_option):
    """The function returns the absolute value of the keyed number"""
    if balling_option>=0
        return balling_option
else:
    return - balling_option
The output of the function will be:
print(my_function(3))
print(my_function(-2))
```

Variable Scope and Lifetime in Python Functions

Variables and parameters defined within a Python function have local scope implying they are not visible from outside. In Python the variable lifetime is valid as long the function executes and is the period throughout that a variable exists in memory. Returning the function destroys the function variables.

Random function in python;

Syntax for Windows

Set PYTHONPATH = c : \python20\lib;

Syntax for UNIX

Set PYTHONPATH = / usr/ local / lib/ python

Scoping and Namespaces

The name of a variable is going to be the identifier that helps Python to find the object.

Namespace is going to be the keys and their values that are going to be tied to the object.

Statements in Python can be used to find variables but only if they are in the local space or the global space.

Local namespaces will ultimately shadow the variables that are in the global space.

Every function that you use in Python has its own namespace. The classes are going to follow the rule that normal functions follow.

Python has the ability to guess where the variable is going to fall. When a variable has a value that is assigned to it, then it is going to be placed in the local space.

A global statement has to be used if you are wanting to put a value to a global variable.

VarName is the signal that tells Python when a variable is global. When this function is used, Python will not look in the local spaces for the function that you are trying to locate.

Example

```
#!/ usr/bin/python

Pennies = 100

Def AddMorePennies ( ):

#this comment is only to tell you that making the
following comment part of the code is going to fix the
code so that it works properly.

#global pennies

Pennies = pennies +3

Print pennies

AddMorePennies ( )

Print pennies
```

Dir( ) function

This function was put into Python so that you can sort out your strings that contain the names of the module that you are currently using.

When a list has the name for all the modules, functions, and variables, they are going to be known as a module.

Example

#! / usr/ bin/ python

#you are going to want the math module for this example

Import math module

Content = dir (math)

Print module content

When Python carries out the command that you have given it, it is going to print out every bit of math that is inside of that module for you to choose from.

name will be the name of the module

file will be where the module is going to be located.

Functions for globals ( ) and locals ( )

These functions are going to be used so that the global and local namespaces are returned but it is going to depend the location in which they are located.

When you are working with the local ( ) function, it will give you the names that are in the function for that particular location.

A globals ( ) function is going to return the names for the function in that global location.

There is a dictionary that has all of the types for both of the functions listed. Names are going to be pulled with the keys ( ) function.

Function reload ( )

Any imported module is going to be carried out once.

Should you want to make the module be executed again, you are going to use the function reload ( ).

This function is going to reload the module that was previously imported.

Syntax

Reload(module_name)

The module name is going to be what the module is named in the Python directory. The string name is not going to be name that is placed in this space.

Example

Reload(South)

Python Packages

There is a hierarchy when it comes to the file directory and this is going to end up defining applications that are in Python.

This package will have sub-subpackages, subpackages, and modules.

Some practice exercises.

Example

#!/ usr/ bin / python

Def Butter():

Print "I am the phone number for the Butter family."

There are going to be two files that have been created with Python that are going to be the same as the example above, however, you are going to have to create a third file so that the correct file is being pulled for the script that you are using.

Functions

Functions are going to be blocks of code that are reusable and are going to only be put in place so that they can execute a single action.

Functions are going to use a higher degree of code that can be used.

Definition of a Function

When a function is defined in Python, it is going to increase the functionality of the function.

There are rules that you have to follow in order to define a function properly.

A statement that has been returned is not going to have any arguments and is going to be returned as none.

Expressions that are returned will end up exiting the function and therefore sending the expression back to the caller.

The keyword def is going to start the block of code and then the name of the function is going to be followed but a set of parentheses.

Each block of code is going to begin with a colon and will be indented at least once space.

The parameters that are set up for the expression will be inside of the parentheses.

For a function, the first statement will be option. Thus making the string a docstring or function string.

Syntax

Def functionname (parameters) :

"function_docstring"

Function_suite

Return [expression]

Python has a default built in that is going to cause the parameters that you set to be positional behavior. If you want them to be different, you are going to need to ensure that you tell Python in which the order that the function is defined.

Example

Def printme (str) :

"This is going to be the string that is placed into the function that I create"

Print str

Return

Chapter 7: Object-oriented programming in Python

Explain & overview object-oriented programming;

Python is an object-oriented programming language. In fact, most modern languages are. But what exactly does this mean? We've spoken in vague terms of objects and classes but we haven't really established quite what this actually means in in any certain terms one way or another.

An object is an instance of a class. Most things you'll deal with in Python are objects. Earlier, when we worked with file input and output, we created instances of a file class. In the last chapter, we were working with strings, and we created instances of the string class. Every instance has built in methods that it can access that are derived from the class definition itself. So what exactly is a class?

A class is a way of defining objects. This sounds terribly vague, but let's look at it this way.

You likely have or have had a pet, right? Let's say there's a dog, and his name is Roscoe.

Well, Roscoe is an animal. Animals have broad, generally defined characteristics, but they're all animals, much like Roscoe is an animal. Get comfy with Roscoe, because we're going to be talking him a lot while we talk about the relations between classes and the relations between classes and objects.

We've established that Roscoe is **most certainly** an animal. He fits the definition of an animal. In this manner, Roscoe is a specific instance of the animal class. If you were writing a simulation of life, and you had people and animals, you would define Roscoe as an instance of **animal**, just as you declared variable **file1** as an instance of **file**, or you declared **tonguetwister** as an instance of **string**.

Now, we need to talk about how we actually define a class and an object within Python.

Create a new file to work with, I'm calling mine pursuitOfRoscoe.py.

Within this file, we're going to start right out the bat by defining a class.

To declare a class, you follow the following template:

class **name**(parent)

We'll talk about parent classes in the next chapter. For now, let's just make our animal class. Every class which isn't deriving from another class has "object" as its parent, so let's put that.

class Animal(object):

We're on our way to defining Roscoe, now. We need a way to define an animal. Let's think about what most animals have. Most animals have legs, that's a start. Animals also have Latin names. Let's work with those two. If your class stores data, you generally need to have an initializer function within your class. It's not a necessity, but it is very common practice.

```
class Animal(object):
def __init__(self, legs, name):
self.legs = legs
self.name = name
```
Perfect. Since Roscoe's a dog, he'll have 4 legs, and his species is Canis Lupus Familiaris.

With that in mind, we now have a definition for animal classes that can be used amongst many animals, not just Roscoe. That's the entire idea behind classes: creating reusable data structures for any given object so that the code is more readable, easy to understand, cleaner, and portable, among other buzzword adjectives that are surprisingly very, very true.

How do we declare an instance of this class now? Like anything else!

roscoe = Animal(4, "Canis Lupus Familiaris")

We can go in and change these variables too. Canis lupus is so formal, and Roscoe's our buddy, so let's change that to Roscoe.

roscoe.name = "Roscoe"

There we go. **Much** better.

Hopefully, this makes the distinction between classes and objects **much** clearer.

Roscoe is a dog, and an animal. Thus he takes from the common concept of being an animal. Since he's an instance of an animal, he automatically receives the traits that all animals have. How cool is that?

Let's go a bit further, and incorporate some functions. What's something that every animal does? Sleep. Every single animal sleeps, aside from Ozzy Osborne.

Let's give animals a function so that they can sleep.

Below our initializer, create a new function called sleep that takes the arguments of **self** and **hours**. Then print out a line of text that says the animal's name and how long it's sleeping for. My code ended up looking a bit like this, and hopefully yours will as well.

```
def sleep(self, hours):

print "%s is sleeping for %d hours!" % (self.name, hours)
```

Then below our declaration of Roscoe, let's go ahead and run the "sleep" function with the argument of 4 hours.

```
roscoe = Animal(4, "canis lupus familiaris")

roscoe.name = "Roscoe"

roscoe.sleep(4)
```

Categories and objects;

Object-oriented programming (OOP) is a model in which programs are organized around objects or data without the use of functions and logic. An object has its unique behavior and attributes. In object-oriented programming, the historical approach to programming is opposed while the stress is given to how the logic is written rather than defining the data within the logic. Examples of objects range from physical entities such as humans to small programs like Widgets.

A programmer focuses on the first step known as data modeling in which all the objects are identified to be manipulated, and these objects relate to each other. The use of frameworks speed up the development, and hence, the development becomes faster, quicker, and more efficient. Most of the web frameworks are available at cheap costs. A framework has strong security implementations. The most benefits of using frameworks are actually due to the community behind them.

In OOP, the developers focus on object manipulation, rather the logic required to manipulate them. This approach is well-suited to programming for the programs, especially the complex, larger, and actively maintained programs. The use of frameworks speed up the development, and hence, the development becomes faster, quicker, and more efficient. Most of the web frameworks are available at cheap costs. A framework has strong security implementations. The most benefits of using frameworks are actually due to the community behind them.

Classes and Objects

It is about the basics that come with the Python code, it is time to move on to our first topic of working with classes and objects. These two topics are important because they will make sure that everything in your code stays in the right place. Your objects are the components which will help define certain parts of the code so that they are organized and easier to understand. The objects all share something in common, and they will be placed into the same class, helping your code to work the way that it should.

There are a lot of things to understand when it comes to working with objects, but the most important part is that whenever you place some objects into the same class, they should have something in common. You can place anything in the same class, but the best way to do this is to place ones that are similar together in the same class. It adds in a little more order to the whole thing. Think about this process as you organizing the closet. You have to make sure that your closet is organized by placing the shoes in one area, hanging up the clothes in another, adding the purses together, and then having a place for all those extra things lying around. You do this process task it ensures that everything looks nice and is easier to find later on.

This is the same idea when you are working on classes. You want to place the similar objects into the same class so that it is easier to find them later on. The program will work more efficiently when these objects are similar, rather than randomly placing unrelated objects into the same class.

To make things easier to understand, you should see objects as different aspects and parts of the code that you are writing and then the classes will be like the containers which you will use to store away these objects. You can easily create a class out of anything that you want and then add in similar objects that match up together into that class. You can pick out whatever label that you want to go with the class, just be certain that it actually makes sense for the type of object that you want to place inside the class. When someone looks at the class, they should have a good idea of what you placed inside of it and the objects should all match that label as well.

If this is a new idea to you and you are just getting started with learning a new coding language, objects and classes are a good place to start because they will help you to learn more while also making sure that everything will stay organized in the code that you are working on. It is your job to learn how to create these classes and then get the objects to go inside of them so that the code works the proper way. Let's take a look at how that is going to work in Python.

How to create a new class

Now that we had a little introduction to these objects and classes, it is time for you to learn the steps on how to create your own class. You have to do this because you will find that it is hard to get started with anything in Python if don't do this first. Once are ready to create the statements that are needed for these classes, you should create a new definition.

You need to place the right keyword first to get this going and then add the name of the class (the name that you are giving to it) right afterward. This will then be followed with a 'superclass' that you will place inside of parenthesis. Another thing that you should consider is that at the end of your first line in Python, you need to add a semicolon. Your code will work without it, but this is considered a part of coding etiquette, so you have to make sure that it is present.

myGenericVehicle.Display_Vehicle()

Before we move on, take the time to open up your text editor and write this code down so you won't forget it. As you work on writing this out, you should notice that there are a few of the basics that we discussed and explained earlier that will show up in this code. You will also see the definition of the object and the method, the destructor function, the different attributes that you will need, and also some regular functions. Since this is the first code that we will have a look at, let's break it down a bit so that you are able to understand and know how to write out codes in this language better.

Syntax object/class instantiation;

This is where you need to write out the object instantiation and then the class definition so that your syntax is proper when put inside the code. These are important because they are the part of the code that will tell your compiler what it should do and which commands are important. If you want to invoke the new class definition inside of the code, you just have to use the 'object.attribute' or the 'object.method()' function and it will work flawlessly.

Special attributes

The next thing that you can focus on in the above code is the special attributes that you want the code to recognize for you. These special attributes will give you some peace of mind because you can know when the attribute will be seen and you can make sure that it is used in the right way to prevent the code from getting messed up. There are a lot of good attributes that can be used in Python, but some of the ones that you really should pay attention to as a beginner include:

__bases__

This is considered a tuple that contains any of the superclasses

__module__

This is where you are going to find the name of the module, and it will also hold your classes.

__name__

This will hold on to the class name.

__doc__

This is where you are going to find the reference string inside the document for your class.

__dict__

This is going to be the variable for the dict. Inside the class name.

How to access members of a class

Now we need to look at how you are able to access members of a class. To make sure that your text editor and compiler are able to recognize a class and execute the parts that you want, you must make sure that this

144

code is properly set up to access all the members of that class. You will be happy to know that there are a few options you can use to make this happen, and all of them will work out well, but the 'accessor' method is the most popular and the most efficient one to work with.

Make sure to open up and place this in your compiler before we move on. If you ask the compiler to run this, you should get some results that show up right away. The results that you get will include that the name of the cat is Frisky (or whatever name you would like to add in there) and that the age is five while the weight is 10. This is the information that we placed into the code, but you can add different names and different numbers in there if that works out better for you. Try out a few different options to see what will work and learn how you are able to make it work for you.

As you can see, classes and objects are really easy to work with. You can create the class and then add the objects that you want and then match it into the class that you created. This will keep your coding nice and organized just like the way that you want it, and it also makes sure the program will actually work.

Methods;

It's impossible to really write a proper introductory crash course on Python and somehow leave out the all-important notion of methods. Methods are prolific. Methods are important. Methods make up the vast majority of Python code and code in general, and they're what makes it possible for code to be reused and for simple functions like list.**append()** to be possible. It's of the utmost importance that you understand what methods are and how they're applied within the world of programming.

What a method basically is is a chunk of code which can be called from other places within the program as many times as you wish. You can choose to send arguments to the method, if you wish, or you can opt to not send arguments to it. Arguments are basically values that are sent to the method for it to manipulate and change however you'd like for it to do so.

Inheritance;

The object-oriented programming (OOP) ensures a higher level of accuracy and reduces time development. Another property of object-oriented programming results in more thorough data analysis. A relation and subclasses build between the objects which can be assigned and allow developers to reuse a common logic while maintaining the unique hierarchy. This property results in more thorough data analysis, high accuracy, and save time.

Encapsulation in python;

The state and implementation of each object are held inside a defined class or boundary but privately. Other objects can only access to this class by calling a list of public functions or lists. Else, the objects cannot access to this class or the authority to make changes. Such programming characteristics of data hiding avoid unintended data corruption and provide greater program security.

Object creation in python;

Open-source organizations also support object-oriented programming by allowing programmers to contribute to such projects in groups that results in collaborative development. Furthermore, the additional benefits of object-oriented programming include the code scalability, reusability, and efficiency.

Principles of Object-oriented programming: There are many principles involved in the object-oriented programming.

Abstraction

The objects reveal the internal mechanisms only. This can be helpful and relevant for the use of other objects. Due to this, the concept of a developer builds that is supportive of going for more addition or making changes over time more easily.

Polymorphism

Depending on the context, objects are allowed to take on more than one form. It is the program that will determine the meaning and usage for each execution of an object, cutting down on the need to duplication code.

Constructors;

Developers criticized the object-oriented programming due to multiple reasons. One of the major concerns about object-oriented programming is that it does not focus on computation or algorithms. Object-oriented programming codes may be more complicated to write and take longer to compile. But developers also find alternatives for such complications. The alternatives include the following:

- Functional programming

- Imperative programming

- Structured programming

However, only the most advanced programming languages enable developers with the options to combine them.

Python as an Object-oriented programming language

Python programming language is widely used as an object-oriented programming language for web application development. According to a survey, 90 percent of the programmers prefer to work with Python language over other languages due to a lot of reasons. Its simplicity, readability and easy interfacing are the major reasons for its preference. Python is used in object-oriented programming as well as follows a procedural paradigm; hence the advanced and diverse applications come out with clean and super simple codes.

Application development with Python programming language also requires some frameworks with the help of which application development is easier for developers. The most used frameworks include Django, CherryPy, Pyramid, Flask, Qt, PyGUI, and Kivy, etc. The use of these frameworks is based on the nature and the requirements of individual projects. The assistance is provided by these Python frameworks to build sophisticated applications with minimal efforts and time.

Python is a popular scripting language for many software development processes. Furthermore, Python can be economically utilized to integrate disparate systems together.

Deleting objects & attributes;

special attributes that you want the code to recognize for you. These special attributes will give you some peace of mind because you can know when the attribute will be seen and you can make sure that it is used in the right way to prevent the code from getting messed up. There are a lot of good attributes that can be used in Python, but some of the ones that you really should pay attention to as a beginner include:

__bases__

This is considered a tuple that contains any of the superclasses

__module__

This is where you are going to find the name of the module, and it will also hold your classes.

__name__

This will hold on to the class name.

__doc__

This is where you are going to find the reference string inside the document for your class.

__dict__

This is going to be the variable for the dict. Inside the class name.

How to access members of a class

Now we need to look at how you are able to access members of a class. To make sure that your text editor and compiler are able to recognize a class and execute the parts that you want, you must make sure that this code is properly set up to access all the members of that class. You will be happy to know that there are a few options you can use to make this happen, and all of them will work out well, but the 'accessor' method is the most popular and the most efficient one to work with.

Make sure to open up and place this in your compiler before we move on. If you ask the compiler to run this, you should get some results that show up right away.

The results that you get will include that the name of the cat is Frisky (or whatever name you would like to add in there) and that the age is five while the weight is 10. This is the information that we placed into the code, but you can add different names and different numbers in there if that works out better for you. Try out a few different options to see what will work and learn how you are able to make it work for you.

As you can see, classes and objects are really easy to work with. You can create the class and then add the objects that you want and then match it into the class that you created. This will keep your coding nice and organized just like the way that you want it, and it also makes sure the program will actually work.

Deleting the entire object.

If you want to delete reference to the Number object, you'll use the word "del" followed by the variable name that you wish to delete. Consider the code below that deletes two variables: age and count that have already been declared and used."

del age, count

Python language supports four different categories of number types. These are:

·   int. when used in a declaration it refers to signed integers. These include those whole numbers that range from 8 bits to 32 bits.

·   long. These are long integers. They can be represented either in octal and hexadecimal numbering notation.

·   float. These are floating real point values. They may range from 8 bits to 64 bits long.

·   complex. These are complex numbers.

Chapter 8: Machine learning with Python

What is machine learning?

Before we can learn more about how to use Python to help with machine learning, it is important to learn more about what the field of machine learning is able to do. Machine learning is a subset of artificial intelligence that will deal with technology being able to learn from the input it is given. With a traditional computer program, the program can only do what was put into the code. It never takes the input from the user or makes any decisions on its own to learn and grow. It simply repeats what the programmer put into the code. But with machine learning, the program is able to learn based on trial and error, by looking at patterns in the data that it sees, and even from the input that the user adds.

The idea behind machine learning is to help the program learn how to read data and then make decisions on its own. There are a lot of times when a program needs to be able to behave without the programmer being there to tell it what to do. For example, with a speech recognition program, the program might have trouble with understanding some speech patterns in the beginning, but over time, it will learn how to understand the person who uses it the most and it will make fewer mistakes.

This is one of the neat things about machine learning. The machine is able to figure out patterns out of a large amount of data, even if the programmer didn't specifically tell it how to behave. This can be helpful in uses such as speech recognition, search engines, and for companies who need to search through large amounts of data to find patterns and make decisions about how to act in the future.

How Can a Machine Learn?

So, the next question is how our machines can learn. Before we dwell on all the details that come with machine learning, we must take a look at the way that humans learn. This is going to give us a good insight into how machine learning is going to work.

For instance, we as humans know that we shouldn't touch a heating plate using our bare hands. But how do we know not to do this? There are two possibilities with this one. Either we were burned in the past by touching one of these plates, or a hot stove, or we were taught by others not to touch these hot plates. In either case, there is some experience in the past that made us not touch the heating plates when we see they are on. In other words, we have some form of past information that we can use to make our future decisions.

Machine learning is going to work in a similar manner. In the beginning, the computer program basically has no knowledge. These programs are just like humans when they are first born, having zero knowledge and not knowing how they are supposed to act. To make a machine learn, information needs to be passed over to these machines. Then going from this information, the machines are able to identify patterns with various techniques. Over time, the machines are going to learn how to identify patterns from the data they have in order to make decisions, and then they can move on to making some decisions with data they haven't even seen.

Training data can be fed into the machine learning algorithms that are nothing but complex mathematical algorithms. The algorithms are then going to result in models for machine learning. These models for machine learning are neat because they have the capability of making predictions on new data, even data that is unseen.

Categories of machine learning

While you may not have heard about machine learning in the past, there are actually quite a few times when it can be used in our modern world. Machine learning is always adding to its teaching set and learning more than we could ever imagine. Some of the ways that machine learning can be used in our modern world include:

- Data Security

Only up to 10 percent of the code changes which is not that much of a change. They have begun to use a learning model that is able to predict what malware is before it can attack. Machine learning algorithms have also been used to look for patterns in how data inside a cloud is accessed and report anomalies that show up and could predict security breaches.

- Personal Security

If you have ever gone to a big event, it's likely that you had to spend some time in a long security line. Machine learning is proving that it is a big asset when it comes to eliminating false alarms and being able to catch things that humans may miss. This could be used at concerts, stadiums, and airports.

- Financial Trading

There are many people who are interested in learning how to predict what the stock market is going to do on any given day so they can make more money. Machine learning algorithms are able to do this with some accuracy. This can help you to estimate how the market is going to react so you can make smarter predictions and keep more money in your pocket.

- Healthcare

Machine learning is able to process more information, as well as spot more patterns, compared to humans.In addition, machine learning can be used in order to understand some of the disease risk factors when looking at a large population. For example, Medecision was able to come up with an algorithm that could identify eight variables that were able to predict hospitalizations that could have been avoided in diabetes patients.

- Marketing Personalization

Even the world of marketing can get in on machine learning. The more that you are able to understand about your customer, the more the company is able to sell. With the help of machine learning, a program can follow where the customers have been on your site, as well as online with other websites, in order to come up with an idea of how to market to that person. This opens up a lot of opportunities in terms of how you can market and reach your customers.

- Fraud Detection

Machine learning has gotten better at being able to spot potential fraud causes in different fields. For example, PayPal is using machine learning in order to catch those participating in money laundering. The company has many tools that they use to compare the millions of transactions that go through and they are able to precisely distinguish between fraudulent and legitimate transactions that occur.

- Recommendations

Many sites, including those like Netflix and Amazon, will use the recommendation feature. This helps them to look through your activity and then compare it with the other users in the hopes of figuring out what you are most likely to binge or watch or purchase next. The recommendations, as they gather more information from users, are always getting better so it won't take long before they meet up with your needs, even if you are a new user.

- Online Search

One of the most popular methods of machine learning is with search engines. Each time that you put in a search, the program is going to watch how you are responding to the results it sends. If you click the top result and you stay on that page for a bit, it will assume that the program got the right results and the search was successful. If you happen to click on the second page, or you go and type in a new search and you don't look at any results, the program is going to learn from that mistake to do better next time.

- Alexa and Other Voice Recognition Software

When you first purchase one of these products, you may run into a lot of issues. It may have trouble recognizing some of your speech patterns and there may be some mistakes. Over time, the program is going to learn from its mistakes and there will be a lot more accuracy in the results you get from the voice recognition program.

As you can see, there are many different uses of machine learning, and this is just the beginning. As the technology continues to change, it won't take long for machine learning to change and adapt with it as well. There are just so many great things that you can do with the help of machine learning, and this is definitely a field that is going to grow into the future.

The Importance of Machine Learning

The ultimate goal of artificial intelligence is to make a machine work in a similar manner to humans. However, the initial work that has been done with this shows that we are not able to make a machine as intelligent as humans. This is because humans are constantly learning in an environment that is evolving all of the time, while this isn't really possible for a machine. Therefore, the best way to make a machine intelligent is to make them learn on their own. What this means is that machine learning is basically the discipline of science that works to teach machines how to learn on their own from data.

The idea that comes with machine learning is that instead of going through and coding all of that logic and data into the program, the data is going to be fed into the machine, and then the machine is able to learn from this data, simply by finding the patterns that are there. What is interesting here is that these machine learning techniques can be faster than humans at finding these patterns.

The techniques that are used in machine learning have been around for some time. But because, until recently, there has been a lack of hardware that is of high performance enough, these techniques were not used to help solve problems in the real world. But now, we have a lot of the complex hardware that is needed for machine learning, and because of the huge amount of data readily available, these techniques are coming back and have been used successfully to help develop machines that are intelligent.

The Different Types of Machine Learning

To keep things simple, the techniques that are used with machine learning are going to be categorized into two different types. These include unsupervised learning and supervised learning. Let's divide these up a bit and see what each one is about.

Supervised Learning

In supervised learning, both the input data, as well as the corresponding category that the input data belongs to is going to be put into the learning algorithm. The learning algorithm is going to learn what the relationship is between the output and the input, and then it can make predictions about the output of any data samples that are unseen.

For example, this kind of learning algorithm can be fed to images of apples that have been labeled as fruit, and the potatoes that are labeled as vegetables. After the machine has gone through training with this data, the algorithm will be able to identify new images of potatoes as vegetable and those of apple as a fruit, even without those labels.

There are a few steps that are often seen when it comes to a supervised learning algorithm. These include:

- You will feed the algorithm with the input records of x, and then the output labels of y.

- For each input record, the algorithm is going to predict an output of y.

- The error in prediction is going to be calculated when you subtract y from y.

- The algorithm is able to correct itself by taking out that error.

- The other steps will continue for multiple iterations until the likelihood of an error is almost gone.

Supervised learning can be used for a wide number of things, but it will usually help you to solve two different types of problems including regression and classification.

- Classification

This is going to refer to the process of being able to predict a discrete output for a given input. So, if the given input is predicting whether your mail is either ham or spam, a tumor is malignant or benign, or if a student is going to fail or pass an exam.

- Regression

In these kinds of problems, the machine learning model is going to be given the task of predicting a continuous value. So, for any given input, it will be able to predict the price of the house or the marks that a student would get on their exams.

Unsupervised Learning

With the unsupervised learning, the algorithms are going to be fed with the input data with no labels. Then the algorithm will learn to identify patterns in the data and can cluster the records that are similar together. Since most of the data a program is going to get will not have labels on it, unsupervised learning is the option that you are more likely to use.

For example, a company may want to use an unsupervised learning algorithm in order to figure out the shopping trends of their customers. This shopping trend could be put into an algorithm for unsupervised learning. This algorithm will take a look at the information and then see if it is able to figure out the future behavior of the customer. The company may use this to find out that someone who often purchases baby products will also purchase milk and then they will move the milk closer to the baby products to get more sales.

This chapter spent some time introducing the ideas of machine learning. We saw a bit more what machine learning is all about, as well as learned that there are some different types of machine learning.

Chapter 9: Python data science libraries and general libraries

With Python, three main libraries are used for basic scientific computing: Numpy for some essential functions, such as fast array structures and matrix operations; SciPy is used for all tasks that may be needed for numerical integration, numerical integration, optimization and statistics, and Matplotlib library for two-dimensional and three-dimensional visualization at a certain level.

In addition to the above-mentioned libraries, there are advanced and stable standard library components for operations such as the manipulation of databases and Internet pages, which are frequently performed in scientific   studies.   In   addition,   comprehensive

```
 1 ▼ def sum_of(F):
 2 ▼      def do(A):
 3              product = [F(a) for a in A]
 4              return sum(product)
 5
 6        return do
 7
 8   sum_of_square = sum_of(lambda a: a**2)
 9   sum_of_inverse = sum_of(lambda a: 1/a)
10
11   c = sum_of_square([1,2,3,4])
12   d = sum_of_inverse([1,2,3,4])
13
```

libraries have been developed specifically to particular disciplines, such as BioPython for biology.

For specific areas of study, the reader can refer to sites such as SciPy for available libraries. In addition, there are practical interfaces for calling languages such as Fortran, C, R from Python that are widely used in scientific computing, link libraries for libraries such as the GNU scientific library, and various libraries for parallel calculations.

The development environment that can be used when making scientific calculations with Python is also very rich: First, of course, general (Python) development tools such as IDLE or Eclipse are available. For scientific developers, there are three different options that provide a more practical environment than MATLAB. Such environments have features such as explor variable explorer u, which is familiar to MATLAB users, and provides possibilities such as changing variables in place, and "object explorer", code analyzer "Pylint, ecek which can be very useful for new learners.

Sage5 or IPython (version> 0.12) can be used to obtain the notebook interface familiar to Mathematica or Maple users. (IPython is a standardized command-line Python environment developed specifically for scientific computing and used as standard. Many other projects (eg Spyder) provide rich interactive programming skills through Python.)

We have briefly mentioned above the use of Python in the field of scientific computing, which is widely accepted. In the remainder of the paper, we will try to show that Python is a good choice of programming languages for scientific computing training in almost all of our universities.

The Python programming language, which is free, was implemented in the standard version using the C language. With these codes, Python's standard library, development tools and many other libraries can be downloaded from the Internet as an open source free of charge and without any license issues. Therefore, all students in scientific computing classes will be able to use these tools freely wherever they want.

In addition, since Python's scientific libraries are open source, they will be able to examine the code of the modules they use for the topics covered in the course and adapt them to different purposes if necessary.

Easy to use Python is designed for easy learnability and use. This easy-to-learn feature is of course an important advantage for any use. In the context of scientific computation, if necessary, it is possible to teach the language to the students from the beginning in scientific computation classes and still give the possibility to devote time to the subjects that are intended to be studied. If students can take the programming courses before they come to their first course in scientific calculation, they will have the opportunity to study more subjects in more depth.

Chapter 10: Machine learning and data science

What is a data scientist?

The funny thing is that this great value of the data contrasts with that precisely the data is the most abundant resource on the planet (it is estimated that 2.5 trillion bytes of new information is created per day). They don't seem easy to make things compatible. How is it possible that something so abundant is so valuable? Even if it was pure supply and demand, accumulating data should be trivial. And it is, the complex thing is to process them.

Until relatively recently we simply couldn't do it. At the end of the 90s, the field of machine learning began to take on an autonomous entity, our ability to work with immense amounts of data was reduced and the social irruption of the internet did the rest. For a few years we have faced the first great 'democratization' of these techniques. And with that, the boom of data scientists: nobody wants to have an untapped gold mine.

In search of a data scientist

The problem is that, suddenly, there has been a great demand for a profile that until now practically did not exist. Remember that you need statistical knowledge that a programmer does not usually have and computer knowledge that a statistician does not usually even imagine.

Most of the time it has been solved with self-taught training that completes the basic skills that the training program should have but does not have. That is why, today, we can find a great diversity of professional profiles in the world of data science. According to Burtch Works , 32% of active data scientists come from the world of mathematics and statistics, 19% from computer engineering and 16% from other engineering.

How to train

Degrees

Today, there are some double degrees in computer engineering and mathematics (Autonomous University of Madrid, Granada, Polytechnic University of Madrid, Polytechnic University of Catalonia, Complutense, Murcia Autonomous University of Barcelona) or in computer science and statistics (University of Valladolid) that seem the best option if we consider this specialization.

Postgraduate

The postgraduate is a very diverse world. We can find postgraduate, masters or specialization courses in almost all universities and a truly excessive private offer. To give some examples we have postgraduate degrees at the UGR, the UAB , the UAM , the UPM or the Pompeu Fabra. However, in postgraduate courses it is more difficult to recommend a specific course. The key is to seek to complement our previous training and, in that sense, diversity is good news.

What we can find in the postgraduate training that we cannot find in the previous training is the ' business orientation ' component. We must not forget that most of the work of data scientists is in companies that seek to make their databases profitable, because what market orientation is highly recommended. In fact, many of the masters in 'big data' are offered by business schools such as OEI or Instituto Empresa.

MOOCS

One of the most interesting resources you can find are the moocs (you know, the massive open online courses). In fact recently, we saw that this self-training option could have a lot of future . Starting with the specialization program in Big Data of Coursera , we can find online courses from the best universities in the world. All this without mentioning the numerous tools to learn languages like Python or R.

What languages should be learned?

In reality, as any initiate knows, in programming the choice of one language or another is always complicated. In this election they intervene from technical or formative factors to simple personal preferences. What is clear is that there are some languages more popular than others.

Although common sense tells us that each language is better for certain things, in practice there is a certain rivalry . Personally, I use R but I usually recommend Python. Not only because it is prettier, but because it is multipurpose and that is always an advantage.

Other tools

A fireproof

- Excel: It is not a language and usually does not like those who work with professional data. Or so they say when asked why polls say otherwise: 59% percent of respondents routinely use excel. So, finally, the application of Office spreadsheets is still a lot of war .

The corporate brother and other languages and programs

- Some languages or environments enjoy some success driven by corporate inertia: it is the case of the classic Matlab but progressively it is losing weight and use up to only 6%.

- If we examine the surveys we can find many more languages that obey more particular needs of the practice of data scientists (or the programs they use): Scala (17%), Slack (10%), Perl (12%), C # (6%), Mahout (3%), Apache Hadoop (13%) or Java (23%).

- Also, although it is possible that we should talk about them separately, there are many specific programs (free or proprietary) that are used in data science with different uses. For example, we could talk about Tableau , RapidMiner or Weka .

The labor market: salaries and opportunities

Salaries, as in general in the world of software development, change a lot depending on the place, the functions and the employer. However, right now it is a well paid expertise . On a general level and according to the annual KdNuggets survey, salaries / incomes average $ 141,000 for freelancers, 107,000 for employees, 90,000 for government workers or in the non-profit sector; 70,000 dollars for work in universities.

However, these average salaries must be taken with great caution. While the average salary in the United States is between $ 103,000 and $ 131,000, in Western Europe it is between $ 54,000 and $ 82,000. In Spain, we are in similar numbers because, despite our (increasingly smaller) deficit of product companies, we have large companies (especially banks) that have turned in this field.

What differentiates data science from the rest of the development world is perhaps the shortage of professionals. This phenomenon makes salaries relatively inflated and, as more dater profiles appear, they adjust. Therefore, it can be said that it is time to get on the wave of data science. Within a couple of years the market will have matured and the opportunities will be elsewhere.

Conclusion

Thank you for making it through to the end of Python Programming. We hope it was informative and able to provide you with all of the tools you need to achieve your goals whatever they may be.

When you have spent some time working on the Python language and you are ready to take your skills to the next level and develop some strong codes that can do so much in just a few lines, make sure to read through this guidebook to help you get started!

Programming is a lot like language learning. You can be a very solid speaker of a language by acting minimally, sure. But it's only by devoting yourself to a language and immersing yourself in it that you'll be able to be hang with the best in terms of your ability to speak that language.

Programming is no different. If you aren't proactive, if you don't get involved in online and real life communities and try your best to program as much as you can in as many new ways as you can find, then you're going to plateau, and you're going to plateau very, very hard.

www.ingramcontent.com/pod-product-compliance
Lightning Source LLC
LaVergne TN
LVHW051236050326
832903LV00028B/2426